BREAK THROUGH, SIS!

DR. KAREN S. RATLIFF

BREAK THROUGH, SIS!

Dr. Karen S. Ratliff / 365 Consulting Group

Break Through, Sis!

Author: Dr. Karen S. Ratliff

ISBN: 978-0-578-44866-4

LCCN: TBD

Contact Dr. Karen S. Ratliff

Social Media

Facebook – I Love Mondays with Dr. Karen

www.ilovemondaysinc.com

This book is dedicated to those who desire to live free

and whole. Allow breakthrough to be your portion.

INTRODUCTION

After overcoming many trials and tribulations, I clearly heard God say, "Daughter of Breakthrough." Difficulty in life and the pursuit of happiness is real but how do we get through tough times? How do we obtain our blessings and the promises of God? I am a firm believer that because we have God's favor, mercy, and grace we are automatically downloaded with the riches of His glory. I also believe, however, sometimes we have to fight for the promises of God.

By experience, research, trials and tribulations, pressures of life, promises of God, mistakes, and mishaps, and continued successes and failures I have learned how to fight for what rightfully belongs to me. God promises us *Blessings* (Proverbs 10:22), *Favor* (Proverbs 3:4), *Good Gifts* (Matthew

7:11), *Increase* (1 Corinthians 3:7), *Wisdom* (James 1:5), *Love* (1 John 4:16), *Power* (Acts 1:8), *Provision* (Luke 12:24), *Strength* (Isaiah 40:29), *Spiritual Gifts* (Ephesians 4:7-13), *Grace* (2 Corinthians 12:9), *Mercy* (Luke 6:36), *Comfort* (Psalm 23:4), *Joy* (Psalm16:11), and our *Heart's Desire* (Psalm 37:4).

God gives us everything that we want, need, and desire, and it is absolutely unacceptable not to receive our promises. Whatever he promised make sure you get it, and anything stolen be sure to take it back. Go forth and recover all. *"And David recovered, all that the Amalekites had carried away; and David rescued his two wives. Moreover, nothing was lacking to them, neither small nor great, neither sons nor daughters, neither spoil nor anything that they had taken to them: David recovered all"* (1 Samuel 30:18-19).

The purpose of this book is to encourage you to move past life's challenges, break through all obstacles, and overcome your trials and fears. Remember, if God did it before, He can do it again. Be not afraid. Go ahead, *Sis, Break Through*!

CHAPTER ONE:

BREAKTHROUGH

Webster's dictionary defines breakthrough as: warfare or an offensive military assault that penetrates and carries beyond a defensive line: an act or instance of moving through or beyond an obstacle: a sudden advance especially in knowledge or technique: a person's first notable success.

If we break the word down, the word, "break" means: separate or cause to separate into pieces as a result of a blow, shock, or strain, interrupt (a continuity, sequence, or course). Breakthrough is an interruption of continuity or uniformity: a pause in work or during an activity or event. The word "through" means: moving in one side and out of the other side of (an opening, channel, or location), continuing in time toward completion of (a process or period).

Breakthrough also means: the act or instance of moving through an obstacle: a sudden, dramatic, an important discovery or development, an instance of achieving success in a particular area.

The Hebrew word for "breakthrough" is *pereṣ* and it means: a gap, a break. It refers to a rupture, a tear, a breaking up or shattering of something: a breach created in a wall of an enemy (2 Sam. 5:20); the breaking or rupture occurring in the process of childbirth (Gen. 38:29). Maybe you need the God of breakthrough to manifest in your life. Is there an obstacle, an invisible wall that blocks your way from walking in everything God has for you?

The breakthrough season is necessary. The purpose of breakthrough is to get you from one place to the next. It is a part of the transitional process. You have to leave a space that is very familiar and move into a totally new space, something new. Transition is also uncomfortable. Breakthrough happens in our lives when God meets us, intercepts, and interjects. Daniel had an encounter with the Prince of Persia. His prayers were held up by Satan. However, God heard Daniel on the first day that he asked for his blessing. Since the first day that you set your mind to gain understanding and to humble yourself before your God, your words were heard (Daniel 10:12).

The will of God is for us to increase, prosper, and breakthrough. When we break through, we experience freedom. Freedom means: the power or right to act, speak, or think as one wants without hindrance or restraint. I believe that God can deliver us from anything. While there are many things God can and will do without our help, there are also some things that we must do to get what God has for us.

God desires to do a new thing within us, but to receive the new, we have to break through some old things. Isaiah 43:19 states, *"See I am doing a new thing. Now it springs up; do you not perceive it? I am making a way in the wilderness and streams in the wasteland."* Many times, we are too busy looking at the obstacles that life has brought us that we can't observe the new thing that God is doing in our lives. We are so caught up in being offended that we are not looking at what God is doing for us. Sometimes God allows us to be offended as an effort to remove someone away from us. It is imperative that we stop in a desolate and quiet space and perceive what God is doing. He promises new things, but if we are blinded and not focused, we will miss it. Can you grasp what God is doing in your life today?

It is normal to be in seasons of trials, tribulations, and bondage. The word of God tells us that we will experience seasons of hurt. In fact, the Scripture states that we will experience a season for everything that we go through in life. We are not exempt from hurt and pain. Ecclesiastes 3:1-9 mentions, *"there is a time for everything, and a season for every activity under the heaven. A time to be born and a time to die, a time to plant and a time to uproot, a time to kill and a time to heal, a time to tear down and a time to build, a time to weep and a time to laugh, a time to mourn and a time to dance, a time to scatter stones and a time to gather them, a time to embrace and a time to reframe from embracing, a time to search and a time to give up, a time to keep and a time to throw away, a time to tear and a time to mend, a time to be silent and a time to speak, and a time for love and a time for war."* We will go through hard times, but after we suffer for a while, God will establish us.

There are areas that God desires for us to receive a breakthrough in. For a breakthrough to occur there are things that we must do. One thing that we can do to experience breakthrough is take action. We can have all of the faith in the world, but until we put some action on what we believe we will remain stuck for a long time.

Experience Breakthrough by Shifting Your Mindset. We must transform our mindset before breakthrough can occur. We have to know that we can break out and break through. We can think of negative things and continue to stay in that negative

9

space, but the word of God tells us to think on good things. Philippians 4:8 states, *"finally, brethren, whatsoever things are true, whatsoever things are honest, whatsoever things are just, whatsoever things are pure, whatsoever things are lovely, whatsoever things are of good report; if there be any virtue, and if there be any praise, think on these things."* When my divorce became final, I left the courtroom thinking that I wouldn't be able to do better or be better. I thought that I would remain alone and in a dark negative space. I had to first believe that I was able to shift from negative to positive. I had to think that I was able to break through that rough time in my life. Sometimes we are stuck in a physical state because our mindset has not shifted. Many of us are afraid to think better because it will require us to change. But once we know better, we have to do better.

We now know that God desires us to have increase, blessings, and promotions. Therefore, our mindsets should shift to those things of God. Proverbs 29:18 states, *"my people perish because they lack knowledge."* We don't die because of lack, murder, or disease. We perish because we are ignorant. Once God exposes His promises to us, we have to believe that we are able to receive them and shift our mindset accordingly. If we grew up living from paycheck-to-paycheck, most often we believe that is the way we should live. We think that is the norm and it is okay. However, when we realize that God desires us to be prosperous and wealthy (Jeremiah 29:11), we should mentally shift to the direction of wealth versus continuing to think on the paycheck-to-paycheck mentality. We can't be afraid to change our mindset from a norm that no longer works for us.

When God is doing a new thing, we have to shift mentally. One of the enemy's tactics is to come against us shifting mentally. He wants us to be distracted with the worries of life so that we don't see what God is doing. God said, *"I am doing a new thing; do you not perceive it?"* meaning that we are missing what He is doing. We have to be intentional about shifting our mind towards His promises. While He is doing a new thing in our lives, don't miss the new by having a mindset on things that are hindering us. Don't miss His new thing by focusing on the distractions. Take heed. Break through and grab on to the new.

Experience Breakthrough by Speaking it into Existence: Once we have in our minds what our new/next should look like, we must then speak it into manifestation. We have to speak our way out of bad situations. What I have is based on what I say. What I spoke years ago, I am now living in it. When I was a senior in high school, I told my friends, "I will be a professor when I grow up." I spoke what I wanted to see. My world currently looks like the words that I spoke almost 20 years ago. In the future, I will be living in a world that my words are currently proclaiming, "I am the head and not the tail." "I am the lender and not the borrower." "I am blessed beyond measure." "I am living under an open heaven." "I have favor with God and with man." "I am a millionaire." "I have consistent streams of income." What I have is based on what I say.

The Bible tells us that if we decree a thing, it shall be established (Job 22:28). The word decree means: an order usually having the force of law: an official order issued by a legal authority: law: A judicial decision or order. I have to decree what I desire to see. Start now by speaking what you desire to see, manifest, shift, and breakthrough.

Life and death is in the power of the tongue (Proverbs 18:21). We can speak things into existence. The problem is sometimes we speak death as well. If you say such things as "this is terrible," "I look ugly," "I hate that person," or "I am going to fail this test;" the truth is it will manifest. You will begin to believe that you are ugly and manifest hatred for a person that you actually love. Because your words have power, it is imperative to watch what you say (when you are speaking negatively) and take authority with what you say (when you are speaking positively).

Experience Breakthrough by Writing the Vision: We are often confused about the definition of vision and sometimes we are confused about if visions and goals are the same. Even though both work hand and hand, these are two different concepts. A vision is having the ability to see. It is the big picture. It is something that may take time to attain and requires small action steps in order to achieve it. For example, purchasing a home, starting a business, and changing careers are all visions that require action steps in order to accomplish them. You should always carry vision. Vision should always be in front of you, and you should always be working towards it (what you see). Creat vision for every area of your life (e.g. physical, financial, spiritual, social, etc.).

We must write the vision and make it plain (Habakkuk 2:2). My home office is covered with vision for every area of my life. I put vision on chart paper that cover every inch of the walls. I see vision every day. I have a focus and understand where I am going by what I wrote. No vision is too small and no vision is too big. God gives vision as far as we can see. He told Abraham, *"I will bless you as far as you can see"* (Genesis 13:15). As far as you can see it, God will manifest it.

It is hard to break through from many situations because we lack vision and don't know who we are. Not knowing who we are, what we were created to be, and why we are on this earth, can damage us throughout our journey in life. If we know our purpose on the earth, we can work daily towards fulfillment in life because we are doing what we are called to do. You can sometimes identify your purpose by acknowledging your passion. I am passionate about assisting visionaries implement their vision and goals by providing strategy, resources, and support. When I am doing that, I am fulfilled. I feel accomplished, and I have a sense of satisfaction.

Experience Breakthrough by Changing Your Surroundings: Who is in your tribe? A tribe is a social division in a traditional society consisting of families or communities linked by social, economic, religious, or blood ties, with a common culture and dialect, typically having a recognized leader. A tribe is needed because it is created to assist with lifting up and pushing you forward in many aspects. A tribe should be diverse and resourceful. It should consist of friends, life coaches, counselors, mentors, mentees, family members, and associates. A tribe is simply a community of people that are for you and willing to encourage, support, and assist whenever necessary. A tribe should consist of at least 5-7 people that you can count on for answers, resources, and/or support. Do they uplift you? Do they encourage you? Do they want to see you free and living a better life?

While looking at your current tribe, you may need to disconnect to reconnect. Disconnect from people who causes pain and hurt and reconnect with those who can help you grow spiritually and naturally. When pregnant Mary and Elizabeth met, their babies leaped. When you connect with like-minded people, your spirit and purpose will leap. Your purpose is ignited. Who is your Mary or Elizabeth? Who is the midwife assigned to you to help deliver your purpose? If two or more stand in agreement, God will hear you (Matthew 18:20). The best way to break through from harmful surroundings is to agree with other positive like-minded people. I heard a prophet once say, "get around your kind." Mary and Elizabeth were different, but the same kind. Get around others who are motivated and excited about God's promises and His love.

Deuteronomy 32:30 explains that one person can put 1,000 to flight and two people can put 10,000 to flight. No matter how large the enemy seems to be or the number of those against you, it only takes one other person to stand in agreement with you and the two of you can outnumber those against you. God is in the midst of two people who agree, *"for where two or three gather in my name, there am I with them"* (Matthew 18:20). Search your tribe and discover at least one person that can stand strong and solid with you on everything that you are petitioning God for. If you don't have anyone in your current circle that you can agree with, get a new circle.

The Bible is clear, *"wherefore seeing we also are compassed about with so great a cloud of witnesses, let us lay aside every weight, and the sin which doth so easily beset us"* (Hebrews 12:1). One way that the enemy tries to attack us is by using negative surroundings. If a drug abuser received treatment and became free from drugs, but went back into the same environment, it is likely that he/she will revert back to his/her old ways because the environment was the same. If you live in an environment of constant negativity and doubt, it will be difficult to remain optimistic about life. The negative environment will try to rub off on you.

Changing your surroundings will change your life and lead you to break through in areas where you struggle. You can't continue to surround yourself with people who are purposeless and visionless, neither should you continue to live in environments that are not healthy. Ask God to make a way to shift people out of your life if they do not belong, and show you another place that is conducive to a healthy environment.

Experience Breakthrough by Ending Things: Understandably, there are a lot of emotions that come with ending things. Because of the unknown in front of us, we are sometimes anxious about the next journey/person that God has for us. The truth is if God is shifting us to the next, it is better than where we came from. Allow God to close doors. When they are closed, don't open them back up. Sometimes God allows people to walk away from us, without reason, and we go back and get them, forcing what is not good to be in our lives. It is hard to break through difficult situations without ending things that got us there in the first place.

I understand that it is hard to shift from our norm, but breakthrough requires change. While a lot of us fear change, change is necessary. First, we bind fear. Don't live in fear. Fear will keep us in bondage. Deuteronomy 31:6, *"Be strong and courageous. Do not fear or be in dread of them, for it is the Lord your God who goes with you. He will not leave you or forsake you."* Headed into your breakthrough, be courageous and know that God has your back. Don't fear the change that is necessary, push through with strength. Ending a thing shows the enemy that you are not playing, so crossover and come out. End it to get to the next and the new. That breakthrough is worth it. End whatever is holding you back from the promises of God. End ungodly relationships and breakthrough soul ties — end cycles. Get on track and stay on course, God is with you.

The Bible tells us that better is an end of a thing than the beginning thereof a thing (Ecclesiastes 7:8). It is better to end a thing than be at the beginning of the next. An old door must close before we can receive what is behind the new door. Close the door to a bad relationship before you walk into a new door with the new person.

Finally, ensure that you celebrate endings. Be glad that things are ending, knowing that you are about to experience better and greater, and end things quickly. As soon as you receive confirmation from God, move forward fast. Don't wait around and don't waste time. You want to be the one ending it on your own, versus God ending it. If He is forced to end something that you should've ended long ago, it will

23

be ended to the point that there is no return and an absolute horrible departure.

Experience Breakthrough by Sowing Your Way Out: Give freely and willingly. Sow your time, money, resources, and energy. God will be pleased. *"The point is this: whoever sows sparingly will also reap sparingly, and whoever sows bountifully] will also reap bountifully. [7] Each one must give as he has decided in his heart, not reluctantly or under compulsion, for God loves a cheerful giver"* (2 Corinthians 9:6-7).

If you are in a rocky marriage, sow into a fruitful one. As a leader, you should sow into an anointed ministry and business. Ask God to show you where to sow for your breakthrough. Sometimes sowing doesn't necessarily mean money, even though it is a common sow. Serving is a part of sowing.

Blessing your leader is a method of sowing. I learned many years ago to never sit in front of my leaders (pastor, mentor, etc.) empty-handed. *"And Isaac sowed in that land and reaped in the same year a hundredfold.*

The Lord blessed Isaac (Genesis 26:12). "As for that in the good soil, they are those who, hearing the word, hold it fast in an honest and good heart, and bear fruit with patience" (Luke 8:15). *"He who supplies seed to the sower and bread for food will supply and multiply your seed for sowing and increase the harvest of your righteousness"* (2 Corinthians 9:10). *"One gives freely, yet grows all the richer; another withholds what he should give, and only suffers want. Whoever brings blessing will be enriched, and one who waters will himself be watered"* (Proverbs 11:24-25). Open your hand and release. God will bless you with even more. God promises the giver blessings. *"Give, and it will be given to you, good measure, pressed down, shaken together, running over, will be put into your lap"* (Luke 6:38). God will take care of the giver. Give freely. Sow your way into breakthrough and the promises of God.

Experience Breakthrough by Seeking Professional Help: Life throws us many unforeseen tragedies. While I believe that God can do all things, including delivering us in an instant, sometimes we need to seek additional counseling. We know that Jesus is the Counselor of all counselors and is the all-wise, True and Living God. *"For to us a child is born, to us, a son is given; and the government shall be upon his shoulder, and his name shall be called Wonderful Counselor, Mighty God, Everlasting*

Father, Prince of Peace" (Isaiah 9:6). While we know that Jesus is the way to the Father and can deliver us from all things, we may also still need professional counseling as well. We need the Father, the Son, the Holy Spirit, and sometimes professional counseling.

My cousin was murdered a while ago, and I just could not get over it. We were really close, and his death took the family by surprise. It literally took me out to the point that I was stuck and walked around in denial. I prayed, cried, fasted, prayed some more, fasted more, and cried more and more. I can definitely say that God comforted and gave me peace about the situation, but there was still a part of me that needed professional help. I needed someone to walk me through the steps on how to heal. I needed to be able to consistently talk to a professional that was non-biased and licensed to assist me.

Professional counselors are necessary to assist with breakthrough. A professional counselor is a person that empowers diverse individuals, families, and groups to accomplish mental health, wellness, education, and career goals. Counselors work with clients on strategies to overcome obstacles and personal challenges that they face.

It is okay to be advised by a counselor. The Bible tells us to seek wise counsel (Proverbs 19:20). There is a serious stigma in many communities that frown upon counseling. Unfortunately, that is a work of the enemy. If professional counselors assist in breakthrough and healing, why is it negative backlash to see one? It is okay to seek counseling, even if it is just to make sure that you are mentally stable.

It is also a good idea to have a professional counselor on standby, just like you have a pastor, friend, and associates nearby. Counselors should be around just in case you need to speak to them. Early on right after my divorce, I went to a counselor to ensure I was mentally solid. Even though I felt and believed that I was in a good space, I wanted to make sure that I was. A professional counselor confirmed that I was doing well after such a dramatic life-changing event. I did not have to guess if I was or not, I sought professional help to ensure that everything was all good. Make sure that you are free in every area, even mentally.

Experience Breakthrough by Having Faith: Faith unlocks doors. Faith allows breakthrough to occur. Hebrew 11:1 states, *"faith is the substance of things hoped for and the evidence of things not seen."*

We should have enough faith to believe that God can get us out of anything that we are not supposed to be in. Honestly, we don't need a lot of faith either, just enough faith that is the size of a mustard seed. *"If we have faith the size of a mustard seed, you can speak to a mountain, and it will be moved"* (Matthew 17:20). God can get us out of any situation that we don't desire to be in if we believe that He can. He can break us through. If we believe that He is God and can do all things, we should believe that He will deliver us from the hands of the enemy. *"Without faith it is impossible to please God"* (Hebrew 11:6). Faith is your access to breakthrough, deliverance, and healing. There was a woman with an issue of blood that was delivered and made whole because she had faith that if she got a hold to Jesus, she would be set free. She stepped out on a mustard size seed of faith, and Jesus made her whole.

> *"And a woman was there who had been subject to bleeding for twelve years. She had suffered a great deal under the care of many doctors and had spent all she had, yet instead of getting better she grew worse. When she heard about Jesus, she came up behind him in the crowd and touched his cloak, because she thought, "If I just touch his clothes, I will be healed." Immediately her bleeding stopped and she felt in her body that she was freed from her suffering.*
>
> *"At once Jesus realized that power had gone out from him. He turned around in the crowd and asked, "Who touched my clothes?" "You see the people crowding against you," his*

31

disciples answered, "and yet you can ask,

'Who touched me?' But Jesus kept looking

around to see who had done it. Then the

woman, knowing what had happened to her,

came and fell at his feet and, trembling with

fear, told him the whole truth. He said to her,

"Daughter, your faith has healed you. Go in

peace and be freed from your suffering"

(Matthew 9:20-22).

Step out on faith. The woman with the issue of blood

believed and stepped out, meaning that she had to

make a move while believing. Sometimes we must

have faith and do something to back up what we

believe God for. *"Faith without works is dead"*

(James 2:14). Would she have received her

breakthrough if she did not touch His garment? What

would have happened if she just stood there thinking,

man, what would happen if I touch Him and did not do anything about it? Faith and works go hand and hand. If you believe God to break a soul-tie, back it up with action. Have faith and submit to a fast. Have faith and stop allowing them to come over at night. Have faith and seek professional advice. God will do His part - will you do yours? Have faith, do your part, and breakthrough.

Experience Breakthrough by Fasting:
Sometimes it is not enough to just pray when searching for a breakthrough. Fasting is intentional abstinence from physical satisfaction. Many times it means to go without food for a period of time in order to achieve a greater spiritual goal. Fasting is intentionally denying the flesh to gain a response from the Spirit. It means renouncing the natural to invoke the supernatural. When fasting, you say "no"

to yourself and "yes" to God. A prayer such as, "God, help me complete this application" versus "God, deliver me from a soul tie" are two different types of prayers. Praying for a soul tie to be broken takes more force, consecration, deliverance and breakthrough strategy. *"Some things only happen with prayer and fasting"* (Matthew 17:21). Some instances and examples to incorporate fasting with prayer:

1. Revelation and instruction: *"While they were worshiping the Lord and fasting, the Holy Spirit said, 'Set apart for me Barnabas and Saul for the work to which I have called them.' So after they had fasted and prayed, they placed their hands on them and sent them off...Paul and Barnabas appointed elders for them in each church and, with prayer and fasting, committed them to the Lord, in whom they had put their trust "* (Acts 13:2-3; 14:23)

2. Grief: *"They mourned and wept and fasted till evening for Saul and his son Jonathan, and for the army of the LORD and the house of Israel, because they had fallen by the sword"* (2 Samuel 1:12)

3. Health concerns: *"David pleaded with God for the child. He fasted and went into his house and spent the nights lying on the ground"* (2 Samuel 12:16).

4. Safety: *"There, by the Ahava Canal, I [Ezra] proclaimed a fast, so that we might humble ourselves before our God and ask him for a safe journey for us and our children, with all our possessions"* (Ezra 8:21).

5. Repentance: *"When they had assembled at Mizpah, they drew water and poured it out before the LORD. On that day they fasted and there they confessed, "We have sinned against the LORD." And*

Samuel was leader of Israel at Mizpah" (1 Samuel 7:6).

6. Breakthrough: *"Is not this the fast that I choose: to loose the bonds of wickedness, to undo the straps of the yoke, to let the oppressed go free, and to break every yoke?"* (Isaiah 58:6).

When I was married, I had a difficult time conceiving, but I had faith that God would allow conception. I stepped out on faith and began to research things that were needed for a new baby. I started eating healthier, literally preparing for the baby that I could not see at that moment. As time went on, while never stopping frequent fasting and prayer strategies, God blessed my womb and I delivered a healthy baby. God was pleased that I had the faith and the works to see the birth of a healthy baby. Faith is necessary for breakthrough, without it, it will be impossible to please God.

Experience Breakthrough by Forgiving: To forgive means to cease to feel resentment against (an offender): to give up resentment of or claim to requital: to grant relief from payment of. It is important to forgive others, forgive ourselves, and forgive what happened in the past. The major reason to forgive people is to ensure that we keep a clean slate with God. God will not forgive us, if we don't forgive others. Matthew 6:14 states, *"forgive others so God can forgive us."* You want a clean slate too, right? There will come a time that we have to forgive people for hurting, abusing, and offending us. Even though it hurts, we have to press in and forgive. Jesus instructed his disciples to forgive "70 times seven times" (Matthew 18:21-22). He also states that, *"if*

there is repentance, you must forgive" (Luke 17:3).
Both scriptures confirm this teaching that He forgives
us as we forgive others.

Forgiveness is not a feeling, it is a choice.
Regardless of what anyone has done to us, we cannot
repay by punishing others. I know this is difficult for
many, especially for me, but the Bible is super clear.
We cannot do wrong to those who wronged us. God
said leave punishment to Him. *"Do not take revenge,
my dear friends, but leave room for God's wrath, for
it is written, "it is mine to avenge; I will repay,"* says
the Lord" (Romans 12:19).

Everyone wants to know how to move on
from tough situations. People act out, hurt others, but
the truth is the only way to really move on, and
breakthrough is to start with forgiveness. Whether
you are learning to forgive yourself for years of

repeated cycles that you've allowed or forgiving the ones you loved for repeatedly disappointing you - there will be a time that you will have to forgive in order to receive your breakthrough. In that moment, you have a choice, suffer and remain in the current situation, or rise above the heartbreak and failure and move forward in life.

The goal should always be better, brighter, greater, and bigger. Think of yourself receiving better. Take a leap and forgive and move on. Move on to greater. Choose to forgive. When you forgive, you gain strength and release bondage. Have the courage to continue on with life with a clean slate with others and with God.

CHAPTER TWO:

THE THREE J'S: JACOB, JOSEPH, AND JOB

JACOB

I am always amazed when I read about Jacob. If anyone, in my opinion, was desperate for a breakthrough, it was definitely Jacob. He pressed in for it. He fought for it, and he would not let go until he received a breakthrough and his blessing from God. Jacob wrestled with God's angel overnight until daybreak. He was absolutely persistent. Have you ever been in a situation where you needed a breakthrough so badly that you had no other choice but to fight? You knew that if you didn't fight, you would either loose or die (spiritually).

Jacob's life started with a struggle. As a twin in his mother's womb with Esau, he fought for

41

position and was born holding on to his brother's heel. Jacob's name is translated as "he deceives" (Genesis 25:26). But when his mother, Rebekah, asked God during her pregnancy what was happening to her, God told her that there were two nations within her womb. God also shared that those two nations (sons) would become divided. One would be stronger than the other, and the older would serve the younger (Genesis 25:23). But God blessed Jacob. God gave Jacob the assurance of His presence.

Jacob's name, "deceiver," summarizes most of Jacob's life. But he was also Israel, one to whom God made promises to which He remained faithful. God appeared to Jacob, and Jacob believed God's promises. Despite Jacob's mishaps and issues, God chose him to be the leader of a great nation that people are still talking about today. We should consider the life of Jacob and know that, in spite of our failings, God can and will use us in His plan. He will still deliver and break us through so that we can continue to be used by Him and to glorify Him.

Even though God blessed Jacob, he still had issues and needed a breakthrough. Just because we have favor with God, doesn't mean we will not struggle from time to time or be without situations that require breakthrough. Even with the blessings of God, we still have to press through for His promises.

> *22 That night Jacob got up and took his two wives, his two female servants, and his eleven sons and crossed the ford of the Jabbok. 23 After he had sent them across the stream, he sent over all his possessions. 24 So Jacob was left alone, and a man wrestled with him till daybreak. 25 When the man saw that he*

could not overpower him, he touched the
socket of Jacob's hip so that his hip was
wrenched as he wrestled with the man. **26** *Then*
the man said, "Let me go, for it is daybreak."

But Jacob replied, "I will not let you go unless
you bless me."

27 *The man asked him, "What is your name?"*

"Jacob," he answered.

28 *Then the man said, "Your name will no*
longer be Jacob, but Israel,[a] *because you*
have struggled with God and with humans and
have overcome."

29 *Jacob said, "Please tell me your name."*

But he replied, "Why do you ask my
name?" Then he blessed him there.

³⁰ So Jacob called the place Peniel,[b] saying,

"It is because I saw God face to face, and yet

*my life was spared" (*Genesis 32:22-30).

Jacob was truly blessed, it was obvious, but he also struggled. However, he didn't stop or give up the fight. He literally fought with the angel until he was blessed. He wrestled until the morning and until he received a breakthrough. Sometimes, we have to show God that we are not going anywhere until He blesses us. We have to prove that we are desperate and willing to fight for His blessings and promises.

Fresh from a divorce I was in a big bind financially. As a single parent and almost everything shifting, my finances took a major turn for the worse. It was very difficult to maintain even the simple bills that I needed to cover. Life was hard. Additionally, I was emotionally and mentally depleted. My health took a turn for the worse, and I just wasn't feeling the joy that my life had to offer me. I was living day-to-day, paycheck-to-paycheck, and mentally exhausted. I had many opportunities to quit and give up, but I pressed in and cried out to God. Like Jacob, I was desperate for God to hear and touch me. I wanted nothing more but for God to show me that He was still with me when everything around me looked dead.

I was hit with so much warfare, but I knew it was because the enemy wanted me to question my decision to divorce. I experienced major warfare with getting into my new home. Every step of the process was extremely difficult, but I continued to push forward with the process. I also needed tax documents in order to close on my home, and every day I spent hours on the phone and in person trying to receive documents that should only take a day to receive. Within 30 days, I had car issue and took my vehicle more than 10 times to the repair shop. It was one issue after another. My back was against the wall. I had two weeks to get out of the house that I rented, and I did not receive my clear to close yet. I was truly faced with warfare that I've never experienced before.

One day I had enough. I cried out to God and went on a fast. I told God that I needed Him and that I understood that it was warfare. During the fast, I prayed with my spiritual parents, sowed money in faith and stood on God's word that I would break free. It only takes one touch. Like the lady with the issue of blood, she believed that with one touch, she would be made whole. It only takes one word. Jesus said, *"Daughter, your faith has healed you. Go in peace and be freed from your suffering"* (Mark 5:34).

She made her move, did what she had to do, didn't give up, and she was freed.

It is important not to give up and watch our confessions. I cried to my spiritual father about giving up on purchasing the home. I was at the end of the rope and felt like giving up. He spoke an encouraging word about not giving up and how God had me. I agreed with it, and within 48 hours I was scheduled to close on my home.

Sometimes we have to get desperate enough to press in and pursue God before we get our breakthrough and blessing. Jacob wrestled with God's angel and told him, "I'm not leaving until you bless me." Basically saying, "we will fight as long and as hard as you want to fight." I didn't have any choice left. Fighting was the only way to get a breakthrough. Jacob could've given up, but he did not. He wanted the breakthrough too badly. Imagine being in a physical fight all night into the early morning. He could've said, "forget it" and went on with his life. But one thing Jacob knew was that if he gave up, his only option was to go back to a life of struggle. There are times in our life where we feel like giving up, throwing in the towel, and completely stop your pursuit a great life. That is normal. It is called being a human being. However, there are also times where you have to fight to get what you deserve.

Have you ever experienced a moment when something was taken or stolen from you? If someone walked up to you today and took your shoes off of your feet and walked away, how would you respond? My initial instinct would be to fight for my things back. I want everything that God has for me. I want all the good things that God has to offer. He promised us good things. *"For the Lord God is a sun and shield; the Lord will give grace and glory; no good thing will He withhold from them that walk uprightly"* (Psalm 84:11). Call me selfish if you want, but I want it all. Everything that God has for me and promised me, I want it. I am willing to fight for it. I am willing to fight for His promises. He promised us life: *"For God so loved the world that He gave His only begotten Son. That whosoever believes in Him shall have eternal life"* John 3:16

He promised us joy: *"The joy of the Lord is my strength"* Nehemiah 8:10

He promised us wealth: *"The blessings of the Lord makes rich and adds no sorrow with it"* Proverbs 10:22

He promised us peace: *Let the peace of Christ rule in your hearts, since as members of one body you were called to peace"* Colossians 3:15

He promised us an abundant life*: "The thief does not come except to steal, and to kill, and to destroy. I have come that they may have life, and that they may have it more abundantly"* John 10:10

He promised that He would take care of us: *Keep your lives free from the love of money and be content with what you have, because God said, "never will I leave nor forsake you"* Hebrews 13:5

His word confirms everything that He promises us. But, just like Jacob, we have to fight to receive the breakthrough, but there is a blessing in the breakthrough.

Jacob fought and received his blessing; *[27] The man asked him, "What is your name?"*

Jacob," he answered.[28] Then the man said,

"Your name will no longer be Jacob, but

Israel,[a] because you have struggled with God

and with humans and have overcome."

[29] Jacob said, "Please tell me your name."

But he replied, "Why do you ask my

name?" Then he blessed him there. [30] So

Jacob called the place Peniel, saying, "It is

because I saw God face to face, and yet my

life was spared" (Genesis 32:27-30).

After the fight, God changed his name. He

changed his circumstances and changed his life for

the better. After my fight, God blessed me with my

home, restored my mind, and gave me double

portions. Press in, fight, and get your breakthrough!

JOSEPH

Joseph is my favorite person in the Bible.
When I think about breakthrough, I think of him. He
broke through from the pit to the palace. He was most
certainly favored by God. Joseph was the cocky child
of Jacob, known as the favorite son because of the
coat of many colors gift that was given to him by
their father. Because of this, his 10 older brothers
schemed against him and sold him to a slave trader.
The older sons told their father that Joseph died
because an animal attacked him. They disliked and
disowned him because he was confident and talked
about his dreams of God's plan for his life (Genesis
37 1:9).

Joseph was sold to a slave trade and taken to
Egypt in a wicked way. This example of Joseph's life

showed that bad things happen to good people. We can be a victim of unwarranted circumstances, but must still find a breakthrough in forgiveness. Because of Joseph's good reputation and his gift being exposed, the king called him to assist with interpreting his dream. His gift made room for him, he used it, and God blessed him with favor from Pharaoh. Pharaoh rewarded Joseph with overseeing the land of Egypt.

All things work together for the good of those who love God (Romans 8:28). We may go through hurt, harm, and pain, even if we did not do anything wrong. However, God has our backs. He will be with us through the process and ensure that we breakout. Joseph served time in jail and had favor while he was there for at least two years. The person in charge of the prison saw Joseph as a good man. He promoted

Joseph to be in charge of all of the other prisoners.

God proved His presence and protection for Joseph.

He will prove His presence and protection for us

through our *prison* season as well.

How do you forgive and breakthrough from

people who hurt you? Joseph did it. He had to in

order to receive his breakthrough and promises of

God.

> [15] *"Realizing that their father was dead,*
>
> *Joseph's brothers said, "What if Joseph still*
>
> *bears a grudge against us and pays us back in*
>
> *full for all the wrong that we did to*
>
> *him?"* [16] *So they approached[a] Joseph,*
>
> *saying, "Your father gave this instruction*
>
> *before he died,* [17] *'Say to Joseph: I beg you,*
>
> *forgive the crime of your brothers and the*
>
> *wrong they did in harming you.' Now,*

therefore, please forgive the crime of the
servants of the God of your father." Joseph
wept when they spoke to him. [18] Then his
brothers also wept,[b] fell down before him,
and said, "We are here as your slaves." [19] But
Joseph said to them, "Do not be afraid! Am I
in the place of God? [20] Even though you
intended to do harm to me, God intended it for
good, in order to preserve a numerous people,
as he is doing today. [21] So have no fear; I
myself will provide for you and your little
ones." In this way he reassured them,
speaking kindly to them" (Genesis 50:15-21).

Joseph received breakthrough and received an
amazing blessing for going through many trials and
forgiving his brothers for selling him to a slave trader.
Not to mention, God reconciled his family and

allowed Joseph to oversee a nation. The brothers suffered from deep regret of their actions, and Joseph forgave them. It was an ecstatic reunion between a grieved father and lost son. Joseph years of unmovable dependency on God, not only, brought about a reunion, but God sat Joseph in a high position so that he was able to save a nation from starvation. What the devil meant for evil, God turned it around and not only blessed Joseph but his entire family as well. Allow God to use you in the midst of a prison season. Still, forgive those who hurt you and watch God break you free.

JOB

When I think of someone that was turned over to the hands of the enemy, lost everything, and God gave them everything back - I think of Job. Have you ever lost anything that God restored? Have you lost a marriage, a home, friends, or a job, and God blessed you with it back? Restoration happens after breakthrough occurs. I know that it hurts, but sometimes God allows Satan to enter into our lives and situations in order for you to stand a test of time. This is what happened to Job. God was bragging about Job's righteousness. Satan insisted that Job was only worthy of God's favor because God's hand was on Job's life. Satan dared God to release his hedge over Job's life and challenged God because he believed Job would curse and deny God. God approved Satan's request. He allowed Satan to impact Job's life, everything except take his life.

Job was wealthy and blameless. He lived a righteous life. God bragged about him. The goal of Satan was to seek who he could devourer, and God said: *"have you considered my servant Job?"* (1 Peter 5:8; Job 1:8). God knew that Job would not curse Him and God also knew that He would bless Him and not allow Job to die.

> *13 "One day when Job's sons and*
> *daughters were feasting and drinking wine at*
> *the oldest brother's house, 14 a messenger*
> *came to Job and said, "The oxen were*
> *plowing and the donkeys were*
> *grazing nearby, 15 and the Sabeans attacked*
> *and made off with them. They put the servants*

to the sword, and I am the only one who has escaped to tell you!"

16 While he was still speaking, another messenger came and said, "The fire of God fell from the heavens and burned up the sheep and the servants, and I am the only one who has escaped to tell you!"

17 While he was still speaking, another messenger came and said, "The Chaldeans formed three raiding parties and swept down on your camels and made off with them. They put the servants to the sword, and I am the only one who has escaped to tell you!"

18 While he was still speaking, yet another messenger came and said, "Your sons and

daughters were feasting and drinking wine at the oldest brother's house, ¹⁹ when suddenly a mighty wind swept in from the desert and struck the four corners of the house. It collapsed on them, and they are dead, and I am the only one who has escaped to tell you!"

²⁰ At this, Job got up and tore his robe and shaved his head. Then he fell to the ground in worship ²¹ and said:

"Naked I came from my mother's womb,
   and naked I will depart.[c]
The Lord gave, and the Lord has taken away;
   may the name of the Lord be praised."

²² In all this, Job did not sin by charging God with wrongdoing" Job 13:22.

God restored Job's health, granting him with twice as much property as before, new children, and successful, long life. Ultimately, Job never cursed God. When Job's wife wanted him to curse God, he refused, *"he replied, you are talking like a foolish woman. Shall we accept good from God, and not trouble?"* (Job 2:10). In all this, Job did not sin in what he said. Be encouraged when you are going through and suffering. Continue to press in for the breakthrough. Like God did for Job, He will restore you.

CHAPTER THREE:

BREAKTHROUGH PHASES: THE BIRTHING PHASE

Mental Shift: The "if" and the "when"

Breakthrough doesn't always need to occur when something painful and dramatic is occurring. Breakthrough can happen after a revelation, shifting, and birthing a vision. There are phases within a breakthrough, similar to birthing a new baby. I call the first phase of breakthrough, or the birthing process, "The Mental Shift." This phase is when a woman (or a man) begins the process of visualizing the possibility of birthing a vision. Something "clicks" and "shifts" in the thought process of seeing a vision. The mental shift doesn't necessarily have to be regarding a child, per se, but whatever the shift, it should start with mentally visualizing the birth of a vision. Maybe it is marriage, launching from a 9-5 into your own business, or even the first time you decide that it is time to get over pain from a lover of the past; whatever the situation is, this phase of the birthing process requires a lot of thought, sitting in silence, hearing from God, and processing information.

For me, I began the birthing process when I was introduced to the thought of starting a family and carrying a child. Having a child was never a thought of "if," it was always a thought of "when." I just knew that when I married, I was going to conceive right away. As a matter of fact, I envisioned having three children. The thought of babies inside of me, carrying them, pushing them on a swing at the playground, and attending their first recitals and football games were always visuals that constantly ran through my mind. I never thought that it would be difficult or even impossible to conceive. That thought never ran through my mind. Again, the only thing that I thought about, in the beginning, was "when" I would conceive. It was all about timing for me. That's why we started trying to conceive immediately after marriage. All of the visuals and the thought processes were right in front of me. I visualized holding my children in the middle of the night, singing love songs, and praying over them while they slept.

My thought process abruptly shifted from "when" to "if" after three years of trying to conceive our first child. I became emotionally drained. My emotional state became more and more frightening. It also didn't help when I constantly heard, "when are you having children?" I avoided the question by saying "whenever God releases them to us." I continued to fight through the thought of possibly never conceiving until I had a vision of my first-born child. In the vision, I saw the face of a brand new baby. The eyes were wide open, and the infant had very curly hair. I knew it was a vision of our baby, but I couldn't tell the sex based on the face and hair alone. I pounded that vision in my heart for a year and then started to get weary again, but it was no turning back at this point. God already showed me the baby in a vision. Whenever my faith started to fade, I asked God if He changed His mind. Another year passed, and He showed me another vision. This time I knew we were having a baby girl. In the vision, she was about four years of age and sitting on the top of

66

the stairs in our home. I pounded that vision in my heart as well. The vision was clear, and I believed God for the release of our child. I just needed to wait for her. That vision carried me for another year, and I cried out to God again and asked Him when He would manifest the visions that I carried for years. I heard Him whisper, "not yet."

Soon after, I received a phone call from my spiritual mother. She said God showed her a vision of a little girl dancing at the altar. God spoke to her and confirmed that I was having a baby girl. I was elated. I pounded that word in my heart. What she spoke to me, I replayed the conversation often. Afterward, the confirmations just kept coming. I was getting my hair done one day, and out the blue, my stylist said, "you are about to conceive." I jumped up out of the chair and started crying and praising God for what was to be. I had faith that she was coming, so I praised God in advance for the breakthrough. Hebrews 11:1 states that *"faith is the substance of things hoped for and the evidence of things not seen."* I did not physically see our daughter at that moment, but I believed, without a doubt, that she was on her way.

Early on, I went to the doctor to see if any problems were preventing us from conceiving a child. The physician confirmed that both of my fallopian tubes were closed and that it was not possible to conceive. But God gave me those visions, and He spoke through people to confirm His promise. I had the faith. I knew that she was coming. The question became what was the work that needed to be done? *"Faith without works is dead"* (James 2:17).

The Bible describes Abraham by mentioning several times some of the great things he accomplished, but Romans four says that he was saved because of his faith. Abraham is known as a man of faith who faithfully followed the Lord's leading. God gave Abraham the promise that Jesus the Christ would come through his family. Abraham and his wife, Sarah was both too old to conceive, but God gave them a child named Isaac. Even though God had promised that Abraham's children would be an awesome nation. God had a plan to allow Abraham to conceive because He knew that Abraham would conceive a great nation through Isaac (Genesis 12:2).

We need faith to receive a breakthrough. God tested Abraham's faith. He asked Abraham to sacrifice his only son, Isaac in Genesis 22. God told Abraham to take Isaac to a mountain to sacrifice him to the Lord. God knew He would stop Abraham from killing Isaac - he just wanted to test Abraham's faith. This was a simple test to prove to us the type of faith Abraham had. Because God showed and told me that I would conceive, I held on to the promise of God. No matter what, I had faith that I would conceive.

After my initial doctor's visit, I had monthly checkups with my doctor. He was able to open one tube via a sharp metal object. I didn't have any drugs, and honestly, he wasn't expecting to see that both fallopian tubes were closed. It was almost unheard of. While he was examining me, he saw that they were closed and just decided to try to open them right away and not wait to give me any meds. The odds were still against me. In the natural, I had a 50% chance of conceiving with the opening of just one of the fallopian tubes.

Still, there was no conception after months of trying. But my faith was still there. I often asked, "okay God, what else do you want me to do?" He then reminded me of the prayer that Hannah prayed;

"One day when Hannah could no longer bear the pain of her empty womb, she went to the temple to present her supplication to the Lord. She cried out to the Lord and wept bitterly. She was so upset that she made a promise to the Lord in her request for a son, she said: "O Lord of hosts, if you will indeed look on the affliction of your servant and remember me and not forget your servant, but will give to your servant a son, then I will give him to the Lord all the days of his life, and no razor shall touch his head." 1 Samuel 1:11

After she said this prayer out loud, she continued to pray in her heart, and her lips moved. Hannah was observed by the priest Eli who accused her of being a drunken woman because she was going so hard in prayer. She explained that she had not had any wine nor strong drink and that instead she was deeply distressed and was praying to the Lord. Eli told her to go in peace and also asked that the Lord would grant her request. After that, Hannah was no longer sad and she no longer fasted. Sometimes, once we receive the word from God, we can take it and know that it will be done.

Not long after her visit to the temple to present her request to the Lord, she was with child. When she delivered her son she called him Samuel, which means, "asked of God." Hannah did not forget her promise to the Lord. As soon as Samuel was weaned, she presented him to the Lord. When she arrived at the temple that same priest, Eli was there. Hannah reminded him of the time that she prayed to the Lord for a son and then dedicated Samuel to the Lord. And he worshiped the Lord there. This was my personal prayer when I decided to conceive. I told God that if He allowed me to conceive, I would dedicate my child back to Him.

Just like my daughter, Kayden, Samuel was born as a gift to the world because of the heartfelt prayer of his mother. Samuel was portrayed as the first prophet and the last judge in the Bible. Additionally, he was an intercessor and prayer warrior, which he learned from his mother. I remember praying a similar prayer stating, "God, if you will bless me with a child, I will give them back to you." Not soon after, I attended a 4am prayer at a church. The pastor instructed the congregation to place three items on a sheet of paper. Those items were to be what we wanted God to do for us. It was a no brainer for me. In fact, I only placed one thing on the index card. The word was "conception." I laid the index card on the altar and watched when the pastor picked it up. He prayed and said, "for those married couples who are trying to conceive, I pray that God will bless you with a child. I pray that, like Hannah, you will give the child back to God." That was the final confirmation that I received before conception. I took that prayer from the man of God and knew that conception was not far off.

The awesome part of that prayer was it was aligned with the prayer that I recently prayed on my own. I had a doctor's appointment scheduled at 8am the same morning. I went to the doctor and took a blood test. She stated that I would have the results of the pregnancy test later that afternoon. I don't know how to explain the way that I was feeling for those hours, but I know that I had the peace of God. I knew that because I heard and saw what He shared with me previously, I was going to conceive. If it wasn't at that moment, it was going to be soon. And God granted my request. The pregnancy test was positive, and my healthy baby was delivered.

Remind God of His word/vision. God gave me three visions of Kayden, and I reminded God of the visions that He showed me. "God, you showed me her. Please manifest her." When He showed, told, and confirmed that I would birth a daughter, I began to prepare for her. I picked out her name, and I started to read pregnancy books. Don't stop the pursuit until

God manifests your promise. Breakthrough and birth it.

PRENATAL CARE: THE PREPARATION PHASE

The promise that you are asking God for may not be conception. Your heart's desire may be to birth something else, something fresh, even something that seems impossible. My plea to you is to move forward with what you desire - your vision and your goals. I do not believe that God will give you a desire and it doesn't manifest. I do not believe that God will show you a promise and don't allow you to birth it. I do not believe that God will show you vision and you are unable to experience it. That is not the type of God that you serve. If He said it, it will be done. If He promised it, it shall manifest. If He showed you, you can take it to the bank because it will happen. Begin to prepare for the vision, just like a parent prepares for a child.

What is prenatal care? Prenatal care is when you receive checkups from a doctor, nurse, or midwife throughout your pregnancy. The prenatal care process helps keep you and your future baby (promise) healthy. Prenatal care is an important part of wellness during pregnancy to ensure that you deliver a healthy baby. Your doctor, nurse, or midwife will monitor your future baby's development and perform routine observations to assist and prevent possible issues. These regular checkups are also a great time to learn how to ease any discomfort you may be having, and learn about your pregnancy and the birth of your future baby (promise).

I was not pregnant but still moved forward with preparing for my child (promise). I started researching the best foods to eat and the best vitamins to take during pregnancy. I stopped eating pork and even stopped getting perms in my hair, due to the possible harm of the chemicals entering my body. I began to look at maternity clothes and always walked in the baby section of every store. I planned and visualized my baby (promise) shower and wrote the names down for my guest list. I prayed about who the godparents would be and visualized my child (promise) being christened.

The prenatal process is the beginning of preparation spiritually and naturally. While your baby (promise) may be different, the process is still the same. You should prepare for the promise before the promise is manifested. If God gave you a vision for a business, you don't just wake up one day, and the business is up and running. You have to prepare for it. You need to develop a business plan, get incorporated, write a mission and vision statement, research competitors, and find a location for it. These are steps to prepare to launch your business and the same way that we plan for childbirth, is the same process of planning to implement your vision (preparation).

STAGE ONE:

The first stage of the birthing process begins when you start having contractions that cause progressive changes in your body, and you are fully dilated. Active labor is when contractions become increasingly intense – more frequent, longer, and stronger. Once you realize that the promise is real and you planned for it, it is time to make it happen by birthing (launching) it.

Stage one of the birthing process also requires a midwife. A midwife is a person trained to assist women in childbirth. *"When she was in severe labor the midwife said to her, 'do not fear, for now, you have another son'"* (Genesis 35:17). Who is your midwife? Who is encouraging you to birth your promise? Who can help you? A midwife comes in all forms, depending on the particular promise that you desire to manifest. Your midwife can be a prayer partner. When at least two people are in agreement with something, God hears them (Matthew 18:20). A prayer partner helps to get a prayer through. They stand in agreement that the visions and goals will come to pass. A prayer partner also intercedes for the visionary. You should meet with your prayer partners at least weekly to petition God for vision and goals implementation.

After my divorce, I was going through consistent warfare, it felt like every day it was

81

something that I had to deal with. I thought because I was going through so much at that time, that maybe me pursuing a divorce wasn't the right thing to do, and that was why I was getting hit so hard spiritually. One of my spiritual mothers prayed with me then said, "I hear the Lord saying, 'I am not upset with you…'". It was confirmation that I was to continue to pursue my divorce, but I also knew that I had work to do spiritually. I had to fight off the major warfare. My spiritual mother was there to pray with me. It helped to know that I had someone with me to help me press in and receive the breakthrough. She carried some of the burdens as well.

Don't get me wrong, sometimes we have to fend for ourselves. Many years ago, I was so used to calling my spiritual mother for her guidance and wisdom. She would pray with me, fast with me, and talk through difficult situations with me. After a fast one day, I was desperately in search of her. I was calling her phone all that day. Finally, I heard God say, "you are strong enough to come to Me directly." Sometimes, God will remove people (temporarily and sometimes permanently) to build our confidence up to seek Him on our own. Don't get me wrong, sometimes we need backup, and the Bible is clear - when two or more are gathered together God is in the midst of them. Two is stronger than one and two can put more to flight, but we also should be confident knowing that God hears our prayers just like He hears those who are interceding for us. David prayed solo and Ezekiel had a full conversation with God regarding the dry bones. They reached God on their own, and God heard and answered them.

Your midwife can be a close friend. Let's face it, everyone needs a friend (or two). Living in a world without friendships can force us to live in a place of bondage, seclusion, and shut in. Friends can be an outlet to express feelings, beliefs, and attitudes. Friends help shape us. Friends are also necessary tribe members. Authentic friends provide critical feedback regarding vision and goals. Friends are also a plus because they typically have background history about our upbringings that can help us make solid decisions. The saying, "friends are either for a lifetime, for a season, or for a reason" is true. But whatever category they are in, they can be a big blessing in helping us move forward in life.

Your midwife can also be a mentor. Mentorship is important because mentors are often transformative for their mentees. Mentors are also usually the catalysts for positive growth and can affect change in ways that others cannot. Research from various scholars indicates that mentoring is connected with a wide range of positive outcomes for mentees. Mentoring has been discussed as a strategy for positive development and as a tool to defuse negative behavior (DuBois & Karcher, 2005). A mentor is an experienced and trusted advisor. They should be someone that a person desires to be like. This person should be in a position that is admirable. One should seek a mentor for many areas of life (e.g., professionally, financially, physically, etc.). A mentor should be willing to "sow" into a person, to help build, encourage, and motivate them. Mentors are also full of resources in a particular area that they are experienced in. A mentor and mentee's relationship should be built on trust, integrity, and discretion.

Mentors should:

1. Understand the mentee's vision and goal: Mentors should really listen for what the mentee is asking. They should ask many questions to get to the "root" of what they need to explore.

2. Strategically plan: Help the mentee with a plan that is aligned with the mentee's goals and hold the mentee accountable.

3. Take action: Help mentees as much as possible. A mentor that believes in their mentee's vision will put their name on the line.

4. Meet the mentee where they are and try to understand the various ways that their needs could be met.

Your midwife can also be a family member. Good, bad, or indifferent, this is one circle that will not change. While there may be some friends and associates who are much closer than family members, the truth is family can't be moved out of this circle, unless its physical distance. Family means "a group consisting of parents and children living together in a household; all the descendants of a common ancestor." This circle helps mold and shape the visionary and vision. The backgrounds, experiences, values, and beliefs are major contributors to visionaries, visions, and the way that vision and goals are implemented.

Your midwife may be someone who encourages you consistently. Surround yourself with people who believe in your vision, goals, and dreams. Allow them to be around you through your success. We need that one person to inspire us with courage. The encourager is similar to a coach. Think of a track coach. They cheer us on while inspiring us to do and be better. An encourager is necessary for your tribe. It could be one word or one push that can launch you into your next season. It is okay to have this person around, especially if you do not do well with encouraging yourself.

A midwife can be a certified life coach. This person can also be a mentor (two for one). A life coach provides step-by-step instructions for completing the vision. They also provide resources to assist with accomplishing goals and tasks. A life coach also researches topics concerning your vision and gathers the necessary information for you to continue to move forward. You should meet with your life coach at least monthly. Many people call themselves a life coach, but not many are certified. A certification is essential because certifications, for the most part, come with training and a ton of resources and connections to help their clients. You can partner with a great life coach by interviewing them. They should be able to highlight their accomplishments, training, and provide resources that benefit you.

Ensure that you have at least one midwife to assist you with your promise. Exodus 17:12: *"When Moses' hands grew tired, they took a stone and put it under him and he sat on it. Aaron and Hur held his hands up—one on one side, one on the other—so that his hands remained steady till sunset."* Proverbs

89

27:17 *"Iron sharpens iron, so one man sharpens another."*

Quote: *"Find people who can handle your darkest truths, who don't change the subject when you share your pain, or try to make you feel bad for feeling bad. Find people who understand we all struggle, some of us more than others, and that there's no weakness in admitting it. Find people who want to be real, however that looks and feels, and who want you to be real, too. Find people who get that life is hard, and who get that life is also beautiful, and who aren't afraid to honor both of those realities. Find people who help you feel more at home in your heart, mind and body, and who take joy in your joy. Find people who love you, for real, and who accept you, for real. Just as you are. They're out there, these people. Your tribe is waiting for you.*

Don't stop searching until you find them." Scott

Stabile

A midwife may also help deliver your

spiritual baby (ministry). They can assist with

nurturing the baby as well by making sure the baby is

healthy. The midwife assists with getting everything

prepared for the baby (ministry) such as a baby

shower and the design of the nursery. Desire a full

term baby (ministry), so it can fulfill purpose and

destiny. Premature ministry is deadly and can destroy

yourself and others. Allow others to assist you with

the birthing of your promise.

STAGE TWO:

Once we make it to the point that we are done

with thinking and planning for the promise, it is time

to push and birth the promise. In this stage of natural

birth, it is time for labor pains to occur and contractions to become closer and closer together. For many of us, the closer we get to our promise, the more the warfare is heightened. The enemy doesn't want us to have anything that God desires for us, so he fights just as hard as we do to try to block us from receiving our promise. If we are not careful to protect our baby (promise) the enemy will force us to abort it, leave it alone, or even damage it.

Moses was a leader of the Exodus, the one God used to deliver His people from Egypt. Moses and God were friends. God Himself buried Moses, and they knew one another face to face. Moses was used by God to perform great deeds in the sight of all Israel. Moses was told about the promise (the Promised Land), used by God to get people to the promise, but was not allowed to enter into the

Promised Land. Imagine spending time praying for your promise, preparing for your promise, and not being able to birth your promise. That is an absolute devastation. No one desires to mentally, physically, emotionally, financially, and spiritually commit to a promise without receiving it.

Moses was not able to see the Promised Land, even though he was a friend of God. In Deuteronomy 32:51-52:

51 This is because both of you broke faith with me in the presence of the Israelites at the waters of Meribah Kadesh in the Desert of Zin and because you did not uphold my holiness among the Israelites. 52 Therefore, you will see the land only from a distance; you will not enter the land I am giving to the people of Israel."

I do not care what is going on, I want God's promises, all of them. It is important to continue to follow God's leading and instruction of birthing promises from the vision to the manifestation. The enemy wants to distract us from birthing a healthy promise so he does all he can to detour or try to abort it. He uses others to demise the plan, but we have to do whatever is necessary to fight for what is ours.

The enemy used Eve to abort a promise from God. Adam and Eve were promised the Garden of Eden, and they were later banned from it, due to Eve's disobedience and listening to the enemy. It happens. Satan sometimes uses great men and women of God to abort, detour, or completely miss what God has for us. None of us are exempt from his schemes or tactics, but the bottom line is we have to remain focused throughout the process. The Bible is clear, our enemy walks to and fro seeking whom he may devour (1 Peter 5:8). His main role of current existence is to steal, to kill, and to destroy us (John 10:10).

We are not only faced with what the enemy throws at us, but we are also faced with the world and our flesh issues. The three (enemy, world, and flesh) are so intertwined that it is hard to tell them apart. In my opinion, however, the major problem is not Satan. I believe that we are our biggest issue. When we know right from wrong, we do not have an excuse to be disobedient, but sometimes we still do and just as our natural parents punished us, there is a punishment from God for our disobedience. The punishment could be the detour, delay, or abortion of the promise(s). Thankfully for us, God is a forgiver and deliverer. He reigns over this world, over Satan, and over us. So if we fall out of the will of God, He can still forgive and deliver us and get us back to His promises.

As a mother who delivered a child naturally, I would also claim that this is the most physically painful stage of childbirth, but one of the most important. We can lose a baby during the second stage if we are not equipped with the necessary tools for delivery. You know you want to start a business, but it may not be successful if you don't have the right tools needed and a midwife to help you.

STAGE THREE:

John 16:21 states, *"when a woman is giving birth, she has sorrow because her hour has come, but when she has delivered the baby, she no longer remembers the anguish, for joy that a human being has been born into the world."* The labor pains hurt, but it is short-lived when the baby is held in your arms for the first time. Similar to the birth of a new vision, after all of the planning, brainstorming, and coaching, once the vision is finally birthed, the difficulty of building is no longer the main focus. Once the breakthrough occurs, we are so happy that God made it happen, the difficulty of getting the breakthrough can almost be forgotten. When God sends a new love, over time the one that hurt you will be an afterthought.

The third stage begins right after the birth of the child/purpose. Now that the first two stages were a success, there's more hard work to do, but this time the work could be for the rest of your life. Similar to having children, our promises and purpose is a lifetime commitment. Because we are born with different gifts, talents, and skills, we should operate and use them to enhance the kingdom of God. The gifts inside of us are ours to keep. Therefore, we should explore them and utilize them as they align with God's will for our life. If I have the gift to teach, I should be operating in that gift in ministry and in the marketplace.

We also have to keep in mind that, at least at the early stages of birth, we have to nurture the promise until we are comfortable with oversight. Once a child grows into adulthood, as parents, the role would change from holding, carrying, and feeding to overseeing and guiding. Similar to a new business, the first few years may require a lot of attention, but as it grows and you get the hang of things, you can oversee it and maybe even hire others to perform day-to-day duties. Master one step at a time - envision your breakthrough, prepare for your breakthrough, and deliver your breakthrough.

Whatever you do, do not ignore or abandon it. You came this far, embrace and hold on to the new thing that God did. If He broke you free from a bad relationship, embrace what is new. If you broke through an unwarranted cycle, be content with your new. Isaiah 43:19 states, *"Behold, I am doing a new thing; now it springs forth, do you not perceive it?"* The new thing has manifested. Your new business, relationship, peace, purpose, or dream is seen in the natural realm. The question is "do you not perceive it?" Sometimes we are so caught up harping on what we left behind or the labor pains that we faced and ignore the new thing that God has already done. Hold tight to the new thing that God performed and allow yourself to let go of the old.

After delivering a baby, you are tired. The same happens after you go through a major breakthrough. Recognize the season that you are in. The problem is we struggle to get from point "A" to point "B" because we are not in the point "B" season yet. The Bible is clear. There is a season for everything and right after a major breakthrough from point "A" to point "B," you may need to get off at the rest stop. You need to rest. After my divorce, God told me to hibernate for the entire winter. I spent an entire winter resting. Get in your secret place, the secret place of the Most High God. That is the safest place you could ever be.

During that time, God was strengthening me. He gave me a new vision and dreams. I had to get rid of all distractions. Every day I sought Him by rising up early and drawing nigh in the late night. I even deactivated my social media accounts. The purpose of that season was for me to get closer, regroup, refocus, and seek a fresh wind, new vision, new revelation, new promises, and updates from heaven. I obeyed God. He told me to rest and get closer to Him. And the first day of spring I received the biggest contract to date. I was obedient. When we obey God, He rewards us.

When Joseph was released from prison, it was to take an elevated position in the government. Joseph knew the region would go through a devastating drought. He made preparations to help save the people. In doing so, he was able to rescue his brothers who had treated him so badly. God rewarded him after he spent time in prison. He elevated him from prison to the palace and the second highest in command. Watch for a promise to manifest after a breakthrough. Joseph trusted in the promises of God. He knew that God had a plan for his life because God showed Joseph his future when he was 17 years of age. Joseph endured difficulties because of his faith in God's Word.

Joseph spent two years in jail but reigned for the rest of his life. Our trouble will not always last so we have to be patient while waiting on God to manifest His promises to us. The promises of God may not come immediately after a breakthrough either. After the breakthrough, be anxious for nothing. God is perfecting those things that are concerning us. *"Be not weary in well doing, but in due season, you will reap if you faint not"* (Galatians 6:9).

God blessed Jacob and gave him a nation (Genesis 32:28, 35:10). Jacob gave Joseph the double portion allotted to the firstborn son. Because the double portion meant that the first son received twice the share allotted to any other son, Jacob promises

Joseph one piece of land more than his brothers

(Genesis 48:22). David recovered all after his

breakthrough (1 Samuel 30:18). And Job was

restored, *"after Job had prayed for his friends, the*

LORD restored his fortunes and gave him twice as

much as he had before." Everyone who had known

him before came and ate with him in his house. They

comforted and consoled him over all the trouble the

LORD had brought on him, and each one gave him a

piece of silver and a gold ring. The LORD blessed the

latter part of Job's life more than the former part. He

had fourteen thousand sheep, six thousand camels, a

thousand yoke of oxen and a thousand donkeys. And

he also had seven sons and three daughters *"* (Job

42:10-13). They suffered, got their breakthroughs,

and kept moving. Once the lady with the issue of

blood pressed in and touched the Master's robe, her life changed forever. We never heard from her again. She pressed, got the breakthrough, and moved on with her life.

Sometimes immediately coming out of a breakthrough leaves us in unfamiliar territories and outside of our comfort zone. I rented a house for a year (prior to I've never rented before). Where I was used to being a landlord, in that season, I was the tenant. I called it my transition home. I had peace there. I heard God very clearly there. I changed my perspective and looked at the situation as launching me into my new season. I could've cursed that place. I even could've blamed my ex, but I didn't. Even though the transition was difficult and I was in an unfamiliar place, I knew God was with me, and I was coming out. I never changed my confession, and I remained in worship and praying posture.

Remain in the presence of God. The safest place in the whole wide world is in His presence. Imagine being in God's hand, safe and sound. No one can pluck you out of it because no one is bigger than God. Press your way into His presence, safety is there, your answers are there and focus on your new beginnings, even if it is not the first new beginning for you. My divorce was not my only breakthrough. I also had to get free and delivered from an ungodly soul tie. We don't have a limit of breakthroughs. If He freed us before, He can free us again. Get your breakthrough as if nothing else matters.

CHAPTER FOUR:

BREAKTHROUGH SCRIPTURES

*"For the word of God is living and active, sharper
than any two-edged sword, piercing to the division of
soul and of spirit, of joints and of marrow, and
discerning the thoughts and intentions of the heart"*
Hebrews 4:12.

*"Who has believed what he has heard from us? And
to whom has the arm of the Lord been revealed? For
he grew up before him like a young plant, and like a
root out of dry ground; he had no form or majesty
that we should look at him, and no beauty that we
should desire him. He was despised and rejected by
men; a man of sorrows, and acquainted with grief;
and as one from whom men hide their faces he was*

despised, and we esteemed him not. Surely he has borne our grief and carried our sorrows; yet we esteemed him stricken, smitten by God, and afflicted. But he was wounded for our transgressions; he was crushed for our iniquities; upon him was the chastisement that brought us peace, and with his stripes we are healed. ... " (Isaiah 53:1-12).

"Therefore, since we have been justified by faith, we have peace with God through our Lord Jesus Christ" (Romans 5:1).

"For I know the plans I have for you, declares the Lord, plans for welfare and not for evil, to give you a future and a hope" (Jeremiah 29:11).

"Praying at all times in the Spirit, with all prayer and supplication. To that end keep alert with all

perseverance, making supplication for all the saints" (Ephesians 6:18).

"From the days of John the Baptist until now the kingdom of heaven has suffered violence, and the violent take it by force" (Matthew 11:12).

"And I tell you, you are Peter, and on this rock I will build my church, and the gates of hell shall not prevail against it" (Matthew 16:18).

"Behold, I am doing a new thing; now it springs forth, do you not perceive it? I will make a way in the wilderness and rivers in the desert" (Isaiah 43:19).

"You let men ride over our heads; we went through fire and through water; yet you have brought us out to a place of abundance" (Psalm 66:12).

"For the Lamb in the midst of the throne will be their shepherd, and he will guide them to springs of living water, and God will wipe away every tear from their eyes" (Revelation 7:17).

"For there are three that bear record in heaven, the Father, the Word, and the Holy Ghost: and these three are one" (1 John 5:7).

"Whoever makes a practice of sinning is of the devil, for the devil has been sinning from the beginning. The reason the Son of God appeared was to destroy the works of the devil" (1 John 3:8).

"Keep your life free from love of money, and be content with what you have, for he has said, "I will never leave you nor forsake you" (Hebrews 13:5)

"No temptation has overtaken you that is not common to man. God is faithful, and he will not let you be tempted beyond your ability, but with the temptation he will also provide the way of escape, that you may be able to endure it" (1 Corinthians 10:13).

"James, a servant of God and of the Lord Jesus Christ, To the twelve tribes in the Dispersion: Greetings. Count it all joy, my brothers, when you meet trials of various kinds, for you know that the testing of your faith produces steadfastness. And let steadfastness have its full effect, that you may be perfect and complete, lacking in nothing. If any of you lacks wisdom, let him ask God, who gives generously to all without reproach, and it will be given him. ..." (James 1:1-27).

*"For the Lord had made the army of the Syrians
hear the sound of chariots and of horses, the sound of
a great army, so that they said to one another,
"Behold, the king of Israel has hired against us the
kings of the Hittites and the kings of Egypt to come
against us"* (2 Kings 7:6).

*"And take the helmet of salvation, and the sword of
the Spirit, which is the word of God"* (Ephesians
6:17).

*"All Scripture is breathed out by God and profitable
for teaching, for reproof, for correction, and for
training in righteousness"* (2 Timothy 3:16).

*"Let the wicked forsake his way, and the unrighteous
man his thoughts; let him return to the Lord, that he
may have compassion on him, and to our God, for he*

will abundantly pardon. For my thoughts are not your thoughts, neither are your ways my ways, declares the Lord. For as the heavens are higher than the earth, so are my ways higher than your ways and my thoughts than your thoughts. "For as the rain and the snow come down from heaven and do not return there but water the earth, making it bring forth and sprout, giving seed to the sower and bread to the eater" (Isaiah 55:7-10).

"No weapon that is fashioned against you shall succeed, and you shall confute every tongue that rises against you in judgment. This is the heritage of the servants of the Lord and their vindication from me, declares the Lord" (Isaiah 54:17).

"Know that the Lord, he is God! It is he who made us, and we are his; we are his people, and the sheep of his pasture" (Psalm 100:3).

"He who opens the breach goes up before them; they break through and pass the gate, going out by it. Their king passes on before them, the Lord at their head" (Micah 2:13).

Meditate on these scriptures when you desire to breakthrough:

"Blessed is the one who reads aloud the words of this prophecy, and blessed are those who hear, and who keep what is written in it, for the time is near" Revelation 1:3.

*"So Jesus said to the Jews who had believed in him,
"If you abide in my word, you are truly my disciples,
and you will know the truth, and the truth will set you
free"* John 8:31-32.

*"Oh give thanks to the Lord, for he is good; for his
steadfast love endures forever! Let Israel say, "His
steadfast love endures forever." Let the house of
Aaron say, "His steadfast love endures forever." Let
those who fear the Lord say, "His steadfast love
endures forever." Out of my distress I called on
the Lord; the Lord answered me and set me free. ..."*
Psalm 118:1-18

*"Of David. Bless the Lord, O my soul, and all that is
within me: bless his holy name! Bless the Lord, O my
soul, and forget not all his benefits, who forgives all
your iniquity, who heals all your diseases, who*

redeems your life from the pit, who crowns you with steadfast love and mercy, who satisfies you with good so that your youth is renewed like the eagle's. .."
Psalm 103:1-22.

"Then the righteous will shine like the sun in the kingdom of their Father. He who has ears, let him hear" (Matthew 13:43).

"Fire devours before them, and behind them a flame burns. The land is like the garden of Eden before them, but behind them a desolate wilderness, and nothing escapes them. Their appearance is like the appearance of horses, and like war horses they run. As with the rumbling of chariots, they leap on the tops of the mountains, like the crackling of a flame of fire devouring the stubble, like a powerful army drawn up for battle. Before them peoples are in anguish; all

faces grow pale. Like warriors they charge; like soldiers they scale the wall. They march each on his way; they do not swerve from their paths. ..." (Joel 2:3-9).

"To the choirmaster: according to Jeduthun. A Psalm of Asaph. I cry aloud to God, aloud to God, and he will hear me. In the day of my trouble I seek the Lord; in the night my hand is stretched out without wearying; my soul refuses to be comforted. When I remember God, I moan; when I meditate, my spirit faints. Selah You hold my eyelids open; I am so troubled that I cannot speak. I consider the days of old, the years long ago" (Psalm 77:1-20).

"For God so loved the world, that he gave his only Son, that whoever believes in him should not perish but have eternal life. For God did not send his Son

116

into the world to condemn the world, but in order that the world might be saved through him" (John 3:16-17).

"The former things I declared of old; they went out from my mouth, and I announced them; then suddenly I did them, and they came to pass. Because I know that you are obstinate, and your neck is an iron sinew and your forehead brass, I declared them to you from of old, before they came to pass I announced them to you, lest you should say, 'My idol did them, my carved image and my metal image commanded them.' "You have heard; now see all this; and will you not declare it? From this time forth I announce to you new things, hidden things that you have not known. They are created now, not long ago; before today you

have never heard of them, lest you should say,

'Behold, I knew them" (Isaiah 48:3-9).

*"For the weapons of our warfare are not of the flesh
but have divine power to destroy strongholds"* (2
Corinthians 10:4).

*"At that time Jesus went through the grainfields on
the Sabbath. His disciples were hungry, and they
began to pluck heads of grain and to eat. But when
the Pharisees saw it, they said to him, "Look, your
disciples are doing what is not lawful to do on the
Sabbath." He said to them, "Have you not read what
David did when he was hungry, and those who were
with him: how he entered the house of God and ate
the bread of the Presence, which it was not lawful for
him to eat nor for those who were with him, but only
for the priests? Or have you not read in the Law how*

on the Sabbath the priests in the temple profane the

Sabbath and are guiltless" (Matthew 12:1-50).

"The words of the Preacher, the son of David, king

in Jerusalem; Vanity of vanities, says the Preacher,

vanity of vanities! All is vanity. What does man gain

by all the toil at which he toils under the sun? A

generation goes, and a generation comes, but the

earth remains forever. The sun rises, and the sun goes

down, and hastens to the place where it rises"

(Ecclesiastes 1:1-18).

"But you will receive power when the Holy Spirit has

come upon you, and you will be my witnesses in

Jerusalem and in all Judea and Samaria, and to the

end of the earth" (Acts 1:8).

"Sanctify them in the truth; your word is truth" (John 17:17).

"This they said to test him, that they might have some charge to bring against him. Jesus bent down and wrote with his finger on the ground. And as they continued to ask him, he stood up and said to them, "Let him who is without sin among you be the first to throw a stone at her." And once more he bent down and wrote on the ground. But when they heard it, they went away one by one, beginning with the older ones, and Jesus was left alone with the woman standing before him. Jesus stood up and said to her, "Woman, where are they? Has no one condemned you" (John 8:6-12).

*"But concerning that day and hour no one knows,
not even the angels of heaven, nor the Son, but the
Father only"* (Matthew 24:36).

*"The vision of Isaiah the son of Amoz, which he saw
concerning Judah and Jerusalem in the days of
Uzziah, Jotham, Ahaz, and Hezekiah, kings of Judah.
Hear, O heavens, and give ear, O earth; for
the Lord has spoken: "Children have I reared and
brought up, but they have rebelled against me. The ox
knows its owner, and the donkey its master's crib, but
Israel does not know, my people do not understand."
Ah, sinful nation, a people laden with iniquity,
offspring of evildoers, children who deal corruptly!
They have forsaken the Lord, they have despised the
Holy One of Israel, they are utterly estranged. Why
will you still be struck down? Why will you continue*

121

to rebel? The whole head is sick, and the whole heart faint" (Isaiah 1:1-31).

"And God is able to make all grace abound to you, so that having all sufficiency in all things at all times, you may abound in every good work" (2 Corinthians 9:8).

"Many shall purify themselves and make themselves white and be refined, but the wicked shall act wickedly. And none of the wicked shall understand, but those who are wise shall understand" (Daniel 12:10).

"And David came to Baal-perazim, and David defeated them there. And he said, "The Lord has burst through my enemies before me like a bursting

flood." Therefore the name of that place is called Baal-perazim" (2 Samuel 5:20).

"Then Death and Hades were thrown into the lake of fire. This is the second death, the lake of fire. And if anyone's name was not found written in the book of life, he was thrown into the lake of fire" (Revelation 20:14-15).

"And my God will supply every need of yours according to his riches in glory in Christ Jesus" (Philippians 4:19).

"I testify again to every man who accepts circumcision that he is obligated to keep the whole law" (Galatians 5:3).

"Now when Jesus learned that the Pharisees had heard that Jesus was making and baptizing more

disciples than John (although Jesus himself did not baptize, but only his disciples), he left Judea and departed again for Galilee. And he had to pass through Samaria. So he came to a town of Samaria called Sychar, near the field that Jacob had given to his son Joseph" (John 4:1-13:38).

"But when Jesus saw it, he was indignant and said to them, "Let the children come to me; do not hinder them, for to such belongs the kingdom of God" (Mark 10:14).

"In the beginning, God created the heavens and the earth" (Genesis 1:1).

"And you will know the truth, and the truth will set you free" (John 8:22).

"Again he began to teach beside the sea. And a very large crowd gathered about him, so that he got into a boat and sat in it on the sea, and the whole crowd was beside the sea on the land. And he was teaching them many things in parables, and in his teaching he said to them: "Listen! A sower went out to sow. And as he sowed, some seed fell along the path, and the birds came and devoured it. Other seed fell on rocky ground, where it did not have much soil, and immediately it sprang up, since it had no depth of soil" (Mark 4:1-41).

"So faith comes from hearing, and hearing through the word of Christ" (Romans 10:17).

"And the Word became flesh and dwelt among us, and we have seen his glory, glory as of the only Son from the Father, full of grace and truth" (John 1:14).

"Give, and it will be given to you. Good measure, pressed down, shaken together, running over, will be put into your lap. For with the measure you use it will be measured back to you" (Luke 6:38).

"Cry aloud; do not hold back; lift up your voice like a trumpet; declare to my people their transgression, to the house of Jacob their sins. Yet they seek me daily and delight to know my ways, as if they were a nation that did righteousness and did not forsake the judgment of their God; they ask of me righteous judgments; they delight to draw near to God. 'Why have we fasted, and you see it not? Why have we humbled ourselves, and you take no knowledge of it?' Behold, in the day of your fast you seek your own pleasure, and oppress all your workers. Behold, you fast only to quarrel and to fight and to hit with a

wicked fist. Fasting like yours this day will not make your voice to be heard on high. Is such the fast that I choose, a day for a person to humble himself? Is it to bow down his head like a reed, and to spread sackcloth and ashes under him? Will you call this a fast, and a day acceptable to the Lord" (Isaiah 58:1-14).

"The revelation of Jesus Christ; which God gave him to show to his servants the things that must soon take place. He made it known by sending his angel to his servant John" (Revelation 1:1).

"And this is the confidence that we have toward him, that if we ask anything according to his will he hears us. And if we know that he hears us in whatever we ask, we know that we have the requests that we have asked of him" (1 John 5:14-15).

"Put on the whole armor of God, that you may be able to stand against the schemes of the devil. For we do not wrestle against flesh and blood, but against the rulers, against the authorities, against the cosmic powers over this present darkness, against the spiritual forces of evil in the heavenly places. Therefore take up the whole armor of God, that you may be able to withstand in the evil day, and having done all, to stand firm. Stand therefore, having fastened on the belt of truth, and having put on the breastplate of righteousness, and, as shoes for your feet, having put on the readiness given by the gospel of peace" (Ephesians 6:11-18).

"Now to him who is able to do far more abundantly than all that we ask or think, according to the power at work within us" (Ephesians 3:20).

"For am I now seeking the approval of man, or of God? Or am I trying to please man? If I were still trying to please man, I would not be a servant of Christ" (Galatians 1:10).

"I appeal to you therefore, brothers, by the mercies of God, to present your bodies as a living sacrifice, holy and acceptable to God, which is your spiritual worship. Do not be conformed to this world, but be transformed by the renewal of your mind, that by testing you may discern what is the will of God, what is good and acceptable and perfect. For by the grace given to me I say to everyone among you not to think of himself more highly than he ought to think, but to think with sober judgment, each according to the measure of faith that God has assigned. For as in one body we have many members, and the members do

not all have the same function, so we, though many, are one body in Christ, and individually members one of another" (Romans 12:1-21).

"Now there were in the church at Antioch prophets and teachers, Barnabas, Simeon who was called Niger, Lucius of Cyrene, Manaen a member of the court of Herod the tetrarch, and Saul. While they were worshiping the Lord and fasting, the Holy Spirit said, "Set apart for me Barnabas and Saul for the work to which I have called them." Then after fasting and praying they laid their hands on them and sent them off" (Acts 13:1-3).

"Peace I leave with you; my peace I give to you. Not as the world gives do I give to you. Let not your hearts be troubled, neither let them be afraid" (John 14:27).

"Whatever you ask in my name, this I will do, that the Father may be glorified in the Son. If you ask me anything in my name, I will do it" (John 14:13-14).

"Truly, truly, I say to you, whoever believes in me will also do the works that I do; and greater works than these will he do, because I am going to the Father" (John 14:12).

"So Jesus said to the Jews who had believed in him, "If you abide in my word, you are truly my disciples" (John 8:31).

"And behold, I am sending the promise of my Father upon you. But stay in the city until you are clothed with power from on high" (Luke 24:49).

"If you then, who are evil, know how to give good gifts to your children, how much more will the

heavenly Father give the Holy Spirit to those who ask him" (Luke 11:13)

"Behold, I have given you authority to tread on serpents and scorpions, and over all the power of the enemy, and nothing shall hurt you" (Luke 10:19).

"And these signs will accompany those who believe: in my name they will cast out demons; they will speak in new tongues" (Mark 16:17).

"Heal the sick, raise the dead, cleanse lepers, cast out demons. You received without paying; give without pay" (Matthew 10:8).

"And he called to him his twelve disciples and gave them authority over unclean spirits, to cast them out, and to heal every disease and every affliction" (Matthew 10:1).

"Will man rob God? Yet you are robbing me. But you say, 'How have we robbed you?' In your tithes and contributions. You are cursed with a curse, for you are robbing me, the whole nation of you. Bring the full tithe into the storehouse, that there may be food in my house. And thereby put me to the test, says the Lord of hosts, if I will not open the windows of heaven for you and pour down for you a blessing until there is no more need" (Malachi 3:8-10).

"Arise, shine, for your light has come, and the glory of the Lord has risen upon you. For behold, darkness shall cover the earth, and thick darkness the peoples; but the Lord will arise upon you, and his glory will be seen upon you. And nations shall come to your light, and kings to the brightness of your rising. Lift up your eyes all around, and see; they all gather together,

they come to you; your sons shall come from afar, and your daughters shall be carried on the hip. Then you shall see and be radiant; your heart shall thrill and exult, because the abundance of the sea shall be turned to you, the wealth of the nations shall come to you" (Isaiah 60:1-22).

"Why have we fasted, and you see it not? Why have we humbled ourselves, and you take no knowledge of it?' Behold, in the day of your fast you seek your own pleasure, and oppress all your workers. Behold, you fast only to quarrel and to fight and to hit with a wicked fist. Fasting like yours this day will not make your voice to be heard on high. Is such the fast that I choose, a day for a person to humble himself? Is it to bow down his head like a reed, and to spread sackcloth and ashes under him? Will you call this a

fast, and a day acceptable to the Lord" (Isaiah 58:3-5)?

"Comfort, comfort my people, says your God. Speak tenderly to Jerusalem, and cry to her that her warfare is ended, that her iniquity is pardoned, that she has received from the Lord's hand double for all her sins. A voice cries: "In the wilderness prepare the way of the Lord; make straight in the desert a highway for our God. Every valley shall be lifted up, and every mountain and hill be made low; the uneven ground shall become level, and the rough places a plain. And the glory of the Lord shall be revealed, and all flesh shall see it together, for the mouth of the Lord has spoken" (Isaiah 40:1-31).

"The rich rules over the poor and the borrower is the slave of the lender" (Proverbs 22:7).

"For he will deliver you from the snare of the fowler and from the deadly pestilence. He will cover you with his pinions, and under his wings you will find refuge; his faithfulness is a shield and buckler" (Psalm 91 3:4).

"I have been young, and now am old, yet I have not seen the righteous forsaken or his children begging for bread" (Psalm 37:25).

"If my people who are called by my name humble themselves, and pray and seek my face and turn from their wicked ways, then I will hear from heaven and will forgive their sin and heal their land" (2 Chronicles 7:14).

"When the Philistines heard that David had been anointed king over all Israel, all the Philistines went

up to search for David. But David heard of it and went out against them. Now the Philistines had come and made a raid in the Valley of Rephaim. And David inquired of God, "Shall I go up against the Philistines? Will you give them into my hand?" And the Lord said to him, "Go up, and I will give them into your hand." And he went up to Baal-perazim, and David struck them down there. And David said, "God has broken through my enemies by my hand, like a bursting flood." Therefore the name of that place is called Baal-perazim. And they left their gods there, and David gave command, and they were burned" (1 Chronicles 14:8-17).

"And David inquired of the Lord, "Shall I go up against the Philistines? Will you give them into my hand?" And the Lord said to David, "Go up, for I

will certainly give the Philistines into your hand" (2 Samuel 5:19).

"Precious treasure and oil are in a wise man's dwelling, but a foolish man devours it" (Proverbs 21:20).

"A good man leaves an inheritance to his children's children, but the sinner's wealth is laid up for the righteous" (Proverbs 13:22).

"The blessing of the Lord makes rich, and he adds no sorrow with it" (Proverbs 10:22).

"Let your eyes look directly forward, and your gaze be straight before you. Ponder the path of your feet; then all your ways will be sure. Do not swerve to the right or to the left; turn your foot away from evil" (Proverbs 4:25-27).

"Honor the Lord with your wealth and with the first fruits of all your produce; then your barns will be filled with plenty, and your vats will be bursting with wine" (Proverbs 3:9-10).

"Delight yourself in the Lord, and he will give you the desires of your heart" (Psalm 37:4).

"You shall remember the Lord your God, for it is he who gives you power to get wealth, that he may confirm his covenant that he swore to your fathers, as it is this day" (Deuteronomy 8:18).

"For we do not wrestle against flesh and blood, but against the rulers, against the authorities, against the cosmic powers over this present darkness, against the spiritual forces of evil in the heavenly places" (Ephesians 6:12).

CHAPTER FIVE:

BREAKTHROUGH WITH THE NEW

"Forget the former things; do not dwell on the past. See, I am doing a new thing! Now it springs up; do you not perceive it? I am making a way in the wilderness and streams in the wasteland" (Isaiah 43:18-19). Ask God to birth the "new" in your life. Confess and decree that God will manifest the "new" in the following areas:

New Beginnings

"For I know that plans that I have for you, declares the Lord, plans to prosper you and not harm you, plans to give you hope and a future" (Jeremiah 29:11).

New Hope

"Hope deferred makes the heart sick, but a longing fulfilled is a tree of life" (Proverbs 13:12).

New Preparation

"Be dressed in readiness, and keep your lamps lit. "Be like men who are waiting for their master when he returns from the wedding feast, so that they may immediately open the door to him when he comes and knocks. "Blessed are those slaves whom the master will find on the alert when he comes; truly I say to you, that he will gird himself to serve, and have them recline at the table, and will come up and wait on them" (Luke 12:35-38).

New Fruit

"I am the true vine, and my Father is the vinedresser. Every branch in me that does not bear fruit he takes away, and every branch that does bear fruit he prunes, that it may bear more fruit. Already you are clean because of the word that I have spoken to you. Abide in me, and I in you. As the branch cannot bear fruit by itself, unless it abides in the vine, neither can you, unless you abide in me. I am the vine; you are the branches. Whoever abides in me and I in him, he it is that bears much fruit, for apart from me you can do nothing" (John 15:1-17).

New Season

"To every thing there is a season, and a time to every purpose under the heaven" (Ecclesiastes 3:1).

Manifestation of The Holy Spirit

"Now there was a man in Jerusalem called Simeon, who was righteous and devout. He was waiting for the consolation of Israel, and the Holy Spirit was on him. It had been revealed to him by the Holy Spirit that he would not die before he had seen the Lord's Messiah. Moved by the Spirit, he went into the temple courts. When the parents brought in the child Jesus to do for him what the custom of the Law required, Simeon took him in his arms and praised God" (Luke 2:25-28).

New Future

"For I know the plans I have for you, declares the Lord, plans to prosper you and not to harm you,

plans to give you hope and a future" (Jeremiah

29:11).

New Changes

"In order to change the course of things your servant

Joab did this. But my Lord has wisdom like the

wisdom of the angel of God to know all things that

are on the earth" (2 Samuel 14:20).

New Days

"A new day will dawn on us from above because our

God is loving and merciful.

He will give light to those who live in the dark and in

death's shadow.

He will guide us into the way of peace" (Luke 1:78-

80).

New Thing

"Behold, I will do a new thing; now it shall spring forth; shall ye not know it? I will even make a way in the wilderness, and rivers in the desert" (Isaiah 43:19).

New Doors

"Thus says the LORD to Cyrus His anointed, Whom I have taken by the right hand, To subdue nations before him And to loose the loins of kings; To open doors before him so that gates will not be shut" (Isaiah 45:1).

New Paths

"My feet has closely followed His steps; I have kept to His way without turning aside" (Job:23:11).

145

New Chapters

"Because of the Lord's great love we are not consumed, for his compassions never fail. They are new every morning; great is your faithfulness. I say to myself, '"The Lord is my portion; therefore I will wait for him" (Lamentations 3:22-24).

Promises

"For all the promises of God find their Yes in him. That is why it is through him that we utter our Amen to God for his glory" (2 Corinthians 1:20).

Divine Connections

"Greater love has no one than this; to lay down one's life for one's friend" (John 15:13).

New Friends

"A man of many companions may come to ruin, but there is a friend who sticks closer than a brother" (Proverbs 18:24).

New Connections

"Faithful are the wounds of a friend; profuse are the kisses of an enemy" (Proverbs 27:6).

New Relationships

"And though a man might prevail against one who is alone, two will withstand him—a threefold cord is not quickly broken" (Ecclesiastes 4:12).

New Clients

"Each of you should use whatever gift you have received to serve others, as faithful stewards of God's grace in its various forms" **(1 Peter 4:10).**

New Mentors

"Older women likewise are to be reverent in their behavior, not malicious gossips nor enslaved to much wine, teaching what is good" (Titus 2:3).

New Mentees

"Then people brought little children to Jesus for him to place his hands on them and pray for them. But the disciples rebuked them. Jesus said, "Let the little children come to me, and do not hinder them, for the kingdom of heaven belongs to such as these." When

he had placed his hands on them, he went on from

there" (Matthew 19:13-15).

New Tribe

"Iron sharpens iron, So one man sharpens another"

(Proverbs 27:17).

New Prayer Partners

"Will you be my prayer partners? For the Lord Jesus

Christ's sake and because of your love for me—given

to you by the Holy Spirit—pray much with me for my

work. [31] Pray that I will be protected in Jerusalem

from those who are not Christians. Pray also that the

Christians there will be willing to accept the money I

am bringing them. [32] Then I will be able to come to

you with a happy heart by the will of God, and we can

refresh each other" (Romans 15:30-32).

New Spiritual Fathers

"Give instruction to a wise man and he will be still wiser, Teach a righteous man and he will increase his learning" (Proverbs 9:9).

New Spiritual Mothers

"A wise man will hear and increase in learning, And a man of understanding will acquire wise counsel" (Proverbs 1:5).

New Counsel

"Seek not counsel from the ungodly.   Seek Godly council from those season saints who you know walk with the Lord" (Psalm 1:1).

New Shepard

And David shepherded them with integrity of heart; with skillful hands he led them" (Psalm 78:72).

New Life Coaches

"Get all the advice and instruction you can, so you will be wise the rest of your life." **(Proverbs 19:20).**

New Territories

"Now Jabez called on the God of Israel, saying, "Oh that You would bless me indeed and enlarge my territory, and that Your hand might be with me, and that You would keep me from harm that it may not pain me!" And God granted him what he requested"

(1 Chronicles 4:10).

151

New Environments

"By faith Abraham obeyed when he was called to go out to a place that he was to receive as an inheritance. And he went out, not knowing where he was going" (Hebrews 11:8).

New Travel

"And he said to them, "Go into all the world and proclaim the gospel to the whole creation" (Mark 16:15).

New Passport

"And people will come from east and west, and from north and south, and recline at the table in the kingdom of God" (Luke 13:29).

New Gatherings

"For where two or three are gathered together in my name, there am I in the midst of them" (Matthew 18:20).

New Journey

"Throughout all their journeys, whenever the cloud was taken up from over the tabernacle, the people of Israel would set out" (Exodus 40:36).

New Experiences

"Therefore, if anyone is in Christ, he is a new creation. The old has passed away; behold, the new has come" (2 Corinthians 5:17).

New Places

"then I will let you dwell in this place, in the land that I gave to your fathers forever and ever" (Jeremiah 7:7).

New Land

"The land which I gave to Abraham and Isaac, I will give it to you, And I will give the land to your descendants after you" (Genesis 35:12).

New Buildings

"By wisdom a house is built, and by understanding it is established, by knowledge the rooms are filled with all precious and pleasant riches" (Proverbs 24:3).

New Property

"Lift up your eyes and look from the place where you are, northward and southward and eastward and westward, for all the land that you see I will give to you and to your offspring forever" (Genesis 13:14).

New Home

"Unless the Lord builds the house, those who build it labor in vain" (Psalm 127:1).

New Sacrifices

"Has the Lord as great a delight in burnt offerings and sacrifices, As in obedience to the voice of the Lord? Behold, to obey is better than sacrifice, And to heed [is better] than the fat of rams" (1 Samuel 15:22-24).

155

New Obedience

"And Samuel said, "Has the Lord as great delight in burnt offerings and sacrifices, as in obeying the voice of the Lord? Behold, to obey is better than sacrifice, and to listen than the fat of rams" (1 Samuel 15:22).

New Consecrations

"The sacrifices of God are a broken spirit; A broken and a contrite heart, O God, You will not despise" (Psalm 51:17).

New Awakening

"Awake, my soul! Awake, harp and lyre! I will awaken the dawn" (Psalm 57:8-11).

New Miracles

"Jesus replied, "What is impossible with man is possible with God" (Luke 18:27).

New Signs

"God also testified to it by signs, wonders and various miracles, and by gifts of the Holy Spirit distributed according to his will" (Hebrew 4:2).

New Wonders

"Therefore they spent a long time there speaking boldly with reliance upon the Lord, who was testifying to the word of His grace, granting that signs and wonders be done by their hands" (Acts 14:3).

New Supernatural Releases

"For the Lord God does nothing without revealing his secret to his servants the prophets" (Amos 3:7).

New Fruit

"So as to walk in a manner worthy of the Lord, fully pleasing to him, bearing fruit in every good work and increasing in the knowledge of God" (Colossians 1:10).

Promotions

"For promotion cometh neither from the east, nor from the west, nor from the south. But God is the judge: he putteth down one, and setteth up another" (Psalm 75: 6-7).

New Promotions

"For promotion cometh neither from the east, nor from the west, nor from the south" (Psalm 75:6-8).

New Blessings

"The blessings of the Lord makes rich and adds no sorrow with it" (Proverbs 10:22).

New Elevations

"Humble yourselves, therefore, under the mighty hand of God so that at the proper time he may exalt you, casting all your anxieties on him, because he cares for you" (1 Peter 5:6-7).

New Money

"Bring the whole tithe into the storehouse, so that there may be food in My house, and test Me now in

this," says the Lord of hosts, "if I will not open for

you the windows of heaven and pour out for you a

blessing until it overflows" (Malachi 3:10).

New Talents

"A man's gift makes room for him and brings him

before the great" (Proverbs 18:16).

New Resources

"I will not withhold any good thing from you" (Psalm

84:11).

New Wealth

"Lazy hands make for poverty, but diligent hands

bring wealth" (Proverbs 10:4).

New Streams of Income

"The man became rich, and his wealth continued to grow until he became very wealthy" (Genesis 26:13).

New Joy

"Nehemiah said, "Go and enjoy choice food and sweet drinks, and send some to those who have nothing prepared. This day is holy to our Lord. Do not grieve, for the joy of the Lord is your strength" (Nehemiah 8:10).

New Laugh

"A joyful heart is good medicine, but a crushed spirit dries up the bones" (Proverbs 17:22).

New Strength

"But those who hope in the LORD will renew their strength. They will soar on wings like eagles; they will run and not grow weary, they will walk and not be faint" (Isaiah 40:31).

New Peace

"You will keep in perfect peace those whose minds are steadfast, because they trust in you" (Isaiah 26:3).

New Happiness

"Go, eat your bread with joy, and drink your wine with a merry heart; for God has already accepted your works" (Ecclesiastes 9:7).

New Freedom

"It is for freedom that Christ has set us free. Stand firm, then, and do not let yourselves be burdened again by a yoke of slavery" (Galatians 5:1).

New Victories

"But thanks be to God! He gives us the victory through our Lord Jesus Christ" (1 Corinthians 15:57).

New Announcements

"But the angel said to them, "Do not be afraid; for behold, I bring you good news of great joy which will be for all the people; for today in the city of David there has been born for you a Savior, who is Christ the Lord. "This will be a sign for you: you will find a

baby wrapped in cloths and lying in a manger" (Luke

2:10-12).

New Celebrations

"Thou wilt shew me the path of life: in thy presence

[is] fulness of joy; at thy right hand [there are]

pleasures for evermore" (Psalm 16:11).

New Ideas

"No man also seweth a piece of new cloth on an old

garment: else the new piece that filled it up taketh

away from the old, and the rent is made worse"

(Mark 2:21-22).

New Business

"He has filled them with skill to do all kinds of

work as engravers, designers, embroiderers in blue,

164

purple and scarlet yarn and fine linen, and weavers—

all of them skilled workers and designers" (Exodus

35:35).

New Businesses

"They were all trying to frighten us, thinking, "Their

hands will get too weak for the work, and it will not

be completed." But I prayed, "Now strengthen my

hands." (Nehemiah 6:9).

New Enterprises

"Any enterprise is built by wise planning, becomes

strong through common sense, and profits

wonderfully by keeping abreast of the facts"

(Proverbs 24:3-5).

New Launches

"Now when he had left speaking, he said unto Simon, launch out into the deep, and let down your nets for a draught" (Luke 5:4).

New Strategy

"If any of you lacks wisdom, let him ask God, who gives generously to all without reproach, and it will be given him" (James 1:5).

New Structure

"The saying is trustworthy: If anyone aspires to the office of overseer, he desires a noble task. Therefore an overseer must be above reproach, the husband of one wife, sober-minded, self-controlled, respectable, hospitable, able to teach, not a drunkard, not violent

but gentle, not quarrelsome, not a lover of money. He must manage his own household well, with all dignity keeping his children submissive, for if someone does not know how to manage his own household, how will he care for God's church" (1 Timothy 3:1-16)

New Skills

"Now send me a skilled man to work in gold, silver, brass and iron, and in purple, crimson and violet fabrics, and who knows how to make engravings, to work with the skilled men whom I have in Judah and Jerusalem, whom David my father provided" (2 Chronicles 2:7).

New Gifts

"Every good gift and every perfect gift is from above, coming down from the Father of lights with whom there is no variation or shadow due to change. Of his own will he brought us forth by the word of truth, that we should be a kind of firstfruits of his creatures. Know this, my beloved brothers: let every person be quick to hear, slow to speak, slow to anger; for the anger of man does not produce the righteousness of God" (James 1:17-20).

New Hobbies

"Whatsoever thy hand findeth to do, do [it] with thy might; for [there is] no work, nor device, nor knowledge, nor wisdom, in the grave, whither thou goest" (Ecclesiastes 9:10).

New Books

"Thus says the Lord, the God of Israel, 'Write all the words which I have spoken to you in a book"

(Jeremiah 30:2).

New Momentum

"For it is God who works in you, both to will and to work for his good pleasure. [14] Do all things without grumbling or disputing, [15] that you may be blameless and innocent, children of God without blemish in the midst of a crooked and twisted generation, among whom you shine as lights in the world, [16] holding fast to the word of life, so that in the day of Christ I may be proud that I did not run in vain or labor in vain. [17] Even if I am to be poured out as a drink offering upon the sacrificial offering of your faith, I

am glad and rejoice with you all. ¹⁸ Likewise you also

should be glad and rejoice with me" (Philippians

2:13-23).

New Solutions

"But if any of you lacks wisdom, let him ask of God,

who gives to all generously and without reproach,

and it will be given to him" (James 1:5).

New Oil

"Then you shall take the anointing oil and pour it on

his head and anoint him" (Exodus 29:7).

New Ministries

"And he gave the apostles, the prophets,

the evangelists, the shepherds[a] and teachers,[b]12 to

equip the saints for the work of ministry, for building

up the body of Christ, 13 until we all attain to the unity

of the faith and of the knowledge of the Son of God, to

mature manhood,[c]to the measure of the stature

of the fullness of Christ" (Ephesians 4:11-13).

New Glory

"For God, who said, "Let light shine out of

darkness," made his light shine in our hearts to give

us the light of the knowledge of God's glory displayed

in the face of Christ" (2 Corinthians 4:6).

New Favor

"So shalt thou find favor and good understanding in the sight of God and man" (Proverbs 3:4).

New Power

"For God hath not given us the spirit of fear; but of power, and of love, and of a sound mind" (2 Timothy 1:7).

New Fire

"He makes his messengers winds, his ministers a flaming fire" (Psalm 104:4).

New Revelation

"The Revelation of Jesus Christ, which God gave unto him, to shew unto his servants things which must

shortly come to pass; and he sent and signified it by his angel unto his servant John: Who bare record of the word of God, and of the testimony of Jesus Christ, and of all things that he saw. Blessed is he that readeth, and they that hear the words of this prophecy, and keep those things which are written therein: for the time is at hand" (Revelation 1:3).

New Dreams

"However, there is a God in heaven who reveals mysteries, and He has made known to King Nebuchadnezzar what will take place in the latter days. This was your dream and the visions in your mind while on your bed" (Daniel 2:28).

New Visions

"Where there is no vision, the people are unrestrained, But happy is he who keeps the law" (Proverbs 29:18).

New Insight

"Indeed, if you call out for insight and cry aloud for understanding, and if you look for it as for silver and search for it as for hidden treasure, then you will understand the fear of the LORD and find the knowledge of God" (Proverbs 2:2-5).

New Assignments

"Only, as the Lord has assigned to each one, as God has called each, in this manner let him walk And so I direct in all the churches" (1 Corinthians 7:17).

New Platforms

"The king stood [on the platform] by the pillar and made a covenant before the Lord -- "to walk after the Lord and to keep His commandments, His testimonies, and His statutes with all his heart and soul, to confirm the words of this covenant that were written in this book. And all the people stood to join in the covenant" (2 kings 23:3).

New Prayers

"This is the confidence we have in approaching God: that if we ask anything according to his will, he hears us" (1 John 5:14).

New Songs

"The LORD is my strength and my shield; My heart trusts in Him, and I am helped; Therefore my heart

exults, And with my song I shall thank Him" (Psalm 28:7).

New Dances

"Let them praise his name in the dance: let them sing praises unto him with the timbrel and harp" (Psalm 149:3).

New Praise

"This is the day that the LORD has made; let us rejoice and be glad in it" (Psalm 118:24).

New Worship

"Worship no god but me" (Exodus 20:3).

New Prophecies

"But one who prophesies speaks to men for edification and exhortation and consolation. One who speaks in a tongue edifies himself; but one who prophesies edifies the church" (1 Corithians 14:3-5).

New Utterances

"The utterances of your lips {you must perform diligently} [just] as you have vowed freely to Yahweh your God whatever [it was] that you promised with your mouth" (Deuteronomy 23:23).

New Decrees

"If you decree a thing, it shall be established" (Job 22:28).

177

New Declarations

"I will declare the decree: the LORD hath said unto me, Thou [art] my Son; this day have I begotten thee" (Psalm 2:7).

New Mandates

"All Scripture is breathed out by God and profitable for teaching, for reproof, for correction, and for training in righteousness" (2 Timothy 3:16)

New Confessions

"If we confess our sins, he is faithful and just to forgive us our sins and to cleanse us from all unrighteousness" (1 John 1:9).

New Courage

"Be strong and of good courage, do not fear nor be afraid of them; for the LORD your God, He is the One who goes with you. He will not leave you nor forsake you" (Deuteronomy 31:6).

New Boldness

"Now when they saw the boldness of Peter and John, and perceived that they were unlearned and ignorant men, they marvelled; and they took knowledge of them, that they had been with Jesus" (Acts 4:13).

New Confident

"I can do all things through him who strengthens me" (Philippians 4:13).

New Beauty

"I praise you, for I am fearfully and wonderfully made. Wonderful are your works; my soul knows it very well" (Psalm 139:14).

New Zeal

"Those whom I love, I reprove and discipline; therefore be zealous and repent" (Revelation 3:19).

New Drive

"I have fought the good fight, I have finished the course, I have kept the faith" (2 Timothy 4:7).

New Appetite

"Ho! Every one who thirsts, come to the waters; And you who have no money come, buy and eat Come, buy

wine and milk Without money and without cost"

(Isaiah 55:1).

New Taste

"Blessed are those who hunger and thirst for

righteousness, for they shall be satisfied" (Matthew

5:6).

New Passion

"And whatsoever ye do, do [it] heartily, as to the

Lord, and not unto men" (Colossians 3:23).

New Wisdom

"Do not forsake wisdom, and she will protect you;

love her, and she will watch over you. Wisdom is

supreme; therefore get wisdom. Though it cost all you

have, get understanding" (Proverbs 4:6-7).

New Understanding

"Whoever is slow to anger has great understanding,

but he who has a hasty temper exalts folly" (Proverbs

14:29).

New Knowledge

"He changes times and seasons; he removes kings

and sets up kings; he gives wisdom to the wise and

knowledge to those who have understanding" (Daniel

2:21).

New Perspective

"As for you, you meant evil against me, but God

meant it for good, to bring it about that many people

should be kept alive, as they are today" (Genesis

50:20).

New Truth

"So Jesus said to the Jews who had believed him, "If

you abide in my word, you are truly my

disciples, ³² and you will know the truth, and the

truth will set you free" (John 8:31-32).

New Growth

"Let your roots grow down into him, and let your

lives be built on him. Then your faith will grow strong

in the truth you were taught, and you will overflow

with thankfulness" (Colossians 2:7).

CHAPTER SIX:

CONFESSIONS

"When I kept silent, my bones wasted away through my groaning all day long" (Psalm 32:3).

Confess your beliefs and say out loud what you desire. God hears you:

I confess that no weapon formed against me shall prosper and when the enemy rises up against me, he is rebuked in the name of Jesus.

I confess, yea, though I walk through the valley of the shadow of death, I will fear no evil: for Thou art with me; Thy rod and Thy staff they comfort me.

I confess that I am walking under an open heaven and the blessings of the Lord that make rich and add no sorrow is my portion.

I confess that the joy of the Lord is my strength and I will rest in God's joy every day of my life.

I confess that new beginnings are my portion. From this day forward, God will make all things new and all things well.

I confess the will of God over my life. I will live a healthy, wealthy, and Godly life.

I confess that I hear God's voice and no other voice shall I follow.

I confess this is the day that the Lord has made. I will rejoice and be glad in it.

I confess no weapon formed against me prosper, in the name of Jesus.

I confess that the Lord God is a sun and shield: The Lord will give grace and glory, and the Lord will not withhold any good thing from me.

I confess that God prepares a table before me in the presence of my enemies and anoint my head with oil; my cup overflows.

I confess that my enemies are exposed and sit under my feet.

I confess that the Lord will make a way out of no way.

I confess that Jesus is Lord and is the only way to God.

I confess that every obstacle is destroyed and every mountain is lowered.

I confess that the wind is at my back and going through life will be easier.

I confess that I am aligned with the will of God.

I confess that the joy of the Lord is my strength.

I confess that joy, wealth, and peace arrest me.

I confess that I have favor with God and with man.

I confess that I am the head and not the tail.

I confess that I am blessed going in and coming out.

I confess that I am a child of God and I receive His protection and blessings.

I confess that I expect the power of God to show up in my life continually.

I confess that I am an oil carrier and have God's anointing that destroys yokes.

I confess that when I open my mouth, God will fill it with His word, truth, wisdom, and knowledge.

I confess that my prayers are answered.

I confess there are no obstacles that I can't overcome.

I confess that I always win.

I confess that lack is never my portion.

I confess that God loves me and I love even my enemies.

I confess that breakthrough is my portion.

CHAPTER SEVEN:

DECREES

"If you decree a thing it shall be established" (Job 22:28). Your words are heard. Decree these things:

I decree breakthrough in every area of my life.

I decree the release of blessing and the overflow of God's promises.

I decree increase in money, resources, and favor.

I decree a shift and fresh wind.

I decree promotions from God.

I decree that every mountain is lowered.

I decree fresh revelation and new beginnings.

I decree that I am the head and not the tail.

I decree that I am above and not beneath.

I decree that the earth yields my possessions.

I decree that where I stand, I possess the land.

I decree that I am healed.

I decree that I am a wealth generator.

I decree that I am free from bondage.

I decree that I am blessed beyond measure.

I decree that I have increased capacity to receive God's outpouring and overflow.

I decree that I have redeemed my time, energy, resources, and connections.

I decree that I have financial breakthrough.

I decree that I have the blessings that make rich and adds no sorrow with it.

I decree that I am whole.

I decree that I am healed.

I decree that I am victorious.

I decree every ordained dead situation around me is revived back to life.

I decree the overflow of God's blessings.

I decree that no weapon formed against me shall
prosper.

I decree that I am healthy, wealthy, and wise.

I decree that I am a child of God and live according to
His purpose for me.

I decree new beginnings and new shifts.

I decree that I birth fruit and God's promises.

I decree that I am arrested with humility and integrity.

I decree that the spirit of oppression is broken off the
operation of my purpose.

I decree that I am justified, completely forgiven, and
made righteous.

I decree acceleration.

I decree multiple streams of income and new
businesses.

I decree the manifestation of God's purpose, plan, and assignments.

I decree miracles, signs, and wonders.

I decree breakthrough in health, wealth, and wisdom.

I decree breakthrough in launching forward.

I decree breakthrough in the spirit and natural realms.

I decree breakthrough in relationships and love.

I decree breakthrough in every area of my life.

CHAPTER EIGHT:

BIND AND LOOSE

We bind and we loose. We have this power so God has already given us the ability to take action and all we have to do is use it. Binding: "to bind tie, fasten; to bind, fasten with chains, to throw into chains, put under obligation, of the law, to be bound to one, to forbid, prohibit, declare to be illicit." When we bind something, we are prohibiting it from occurring.

Loosing: "to loose any person (or thing) tied fastened; bandages of the feet, the shoes, to loose one bound, unbind, release from bonds, set free, of one bound up, discharge from prison, let go, and to dismiss." Therefore, loosing is the opposite action.

You are untying something by loosening it. You are setting it free.

"What so ever you bind on earth will be bound in heaven. And whatsoever you loose on earth, will be loosed in heaven" (Matthew 18:18). Your words have power to bind and loose it:

I bind Satan's hands and shut his mouth and loose the angels of the Lord around me.

I bind poverty and loose my wealth.

I bind sickness and loose perfect health.

I bind the spirit of manipulation and loose the spirit of freedom.

I bind anxiety and loose calmness.

I bind confusion and loose a peace of mind.

I bind frustration and loose joy.

I bind hate and loose love.

I bind storms and I loose peace.

I bind detour and loose the spirit of pursuit.

I bind the spirit of delay and loose the spirit of promotion.

I bind the spirit of abortion and loose the spirit of conception.

I bind the spirit of loneliness and loose the spirit of liberation.

I bind warfare and loose harmony.

I bind debt and loose wealth.

I bind death and loose life.

I bind addiction and loose discipline.

I bind weakness and loose strength.

I bind a lying spirit and loose the truth.

I bind grief and loose joy.

I bind depression and loose joy.

I bind sin and loose righteousness.

I bind the enemy and loose God's presence.

I bind the spirit of torture and turmoil and loose the blood of Jesus.

I bind the enemy's tactics and loose God's purpose and destiny.

I bind opposition and loose a submissive spirit.

I bind the spirit of divorce and loose the spirit of reconciliation.

I bind the spirit of offense and loose the spirit of kindness.

I bind the spirit of unhappiness and loose the spirit of happiness.

I bind the spirit of greed and loose the spirit of generosity.

CHAPTER NINE:

BREAKTHROUGH PRAYER

"For where two or three gather in my name, there am I with them" (Matthew 18:20).

"Our Father, who is in heaven, hallowed by thy name; thy kingdom come, thy will be done, on earth as it is in heaven. Give us this day, our daily bread. Forgive us as we forgive those who trespass against us. Lead us not into temptation, but deliver us from evil" (Matthew 6:9-13).

Father, we come before you to bless your name. Your word says to enter into your gates with thanksgiving and your courts with praise. Therefore, we praise you and magnify your name. We thank you for sitting high and looking low. We praise you for being exactly who you say you are. Thank you for keeping us, guiding us, and protecting us. Thank you for your everlasting love. Thank you for hearing our cry and healing our broken hearts. Thank you for manifesting your promises. Thank you for thinking about us, holding us close, and covering us from danger seen and unseen. Thank you for going before us and calling us to you. Thank you for making every crooked place straight and every mountain lowered. Thank you for putting the wind against our back to make the journey of life easier. Thank you for what you have done, is doing, and will do. Thank you for miracles, signs, and wonders. Thank you for a hedge of protection. Thank you for favor with you and favor with man. Thank you for open doors and increase. Thank you for an open heaven! God, you are good, and you do all things well. You are good, and your mercies endure forever. God, you are good, and you do not withhold any good thing from us. You are a good, good Father and it is an honor to bless your name. It is an honor to sing praises to you. It is an honor to serve and obey you.

You are the Alpha and the Omega. You are the Beginning and the End. You are the Way Maker and the Yoke Breaker. You are the True and Living God. You are the Messiah, Elohim, and the Creator. You are Abba Father. You are El Roi, the God who sees. You are El Shaddai, the God Almighty. You are Yahweh, the Self-Existent One. We worship, magnify, glorify, honor, and adore you. We salute you, we bow before you. Your name alone is great. Your name alone is Mighty. Your name alone destroys yokes. Your name alone sets free. Your name alone breaks us through and as the angels cry, Holy, Holy, Holy, we sing a Hallelujah praise.

God, we ask that you forgive us of our sins. We confess that we have all sinned and fallen short of your glory. We ask that you wipe us clear and make us pure. God purify us from our sins and make us whole. We confess our sins and ask that you will forgive and forget those things that we have done that were not pleasing in your sight. We ask that you forgive us for the sins done knowingly and unknowingly. God, we forgive all of those who did us wrong and pray that those who we did wrong will forgive us. God, we are in Christ. Therefore, we are a new creature and redeemed by the blood of Jesus. Even though we have sinned against you, you are merciful and forgiving (Daniel 9:9). Thank you for rescuing us from darkness and bringing us back into the kingdom, in whom we have redemption, the forgiveness of sins (Colossians 1:13-14). As far as the east is from the west, so far have you removed our transgressions from us (Psalm 103:12). God, we thank you for a clean slate and a new beginning. Thank you for not throwing our past mistakes in my face. Thank you for not even remembering our sins. Thank you for being for us and not against us, even when we don't deserve it. Thank you for blessing us, even when we purposefully do wrong things. Thank you for your everlasting love and kindness towards your sons and daughters. We need You. Thank you for not holding out on us. God, show us where we stand with you. Show us when we are right and when we are wrong. Clean us up and give us a clean slate. Show us the way to go. We desire to please you, we desire to know you more intimately and bind anything that would get in the way of us getting closer to you.

We bind the hands of the enemy and shut his mouth. We loose the blood of Jesus and the blessings that makes rich and adds no sorrow with it (Proverbs 10:22). No weapon formed against us shall prosper, in the name of Jesus (Isaiah 54:17). We bind backlash, retaliation, and destruction, and we loose God's shield. We bind every demonic attack of the enemy and loose God's angels all around us. Satan, we rebuke you, the blood of Jesus is against you. You have no authority over us. As a matter of fact, we have authority over you. We have the authority to trample over serpents and scorpions, and all of the power of the enemy; nothing shall by any means hurt or harm us (Luke 10:19). By the power of God, we destroy every generational curses, strongholds, and soul tie, in the name of Jesus.

God, we ask specifically for you to break all distractions that will not allow us to get closer to you. You said to *"knock, and the door shall be open, seek and we shall find, ask and it shall be given"* (Matthew 7:7).

Lord, we desire breakthrough concerning generational curses.

We desire breakthrough concerning debt and financial burdens.

We desire breakthrough concerning soul-ties.

We desire breakthrough concerning ongoing and unnecessary warfare.

We desire breakthrough concerning unwarranted cycles.

We desire breakthrough concerning sexual sin.

We desire breakthrough concerning illnesses and diseases.

We desire breakthrough concerning poverty and demotions.

We desire breakthrough concerning our children and family.

We desire breakthrough concerning toxic and ungodly relationships.

We desire breakthrough concerning our jobs.

We desire breakthrough concerning promotion, expansion, and enlargement.

We desire breakthrough concerning our prayer life.

We desire breakthrough concerning our spiritual state.

We desire breakthrough concerning our emotions.

We desire breakthrough concerning marriage and relationships.

We desire breakthrough concerning our wealth.

We desire breakthrough concerning our businesses.

We desire breakthrough concerning our purpose, destiny, and assignment.

We desire breakthrough concerning our community and culture.

We desire breakthrough concerning our unbelief.

We desire breakthrough concerning us being impatience.

We desire breakthrough concerning forgiveness.

God, you are faithful! The fight is real, but victory, in the end, is real as well. We refuse to call ourselves Christians and live an entire life defeated. Satan is a big fat liar! We decree and declare that we received breakthrough in every area of our life, in the name of Jesus. We prophesy that the fire of God hits our home and scatters the enemy! We will live in victory. We will receive the promises of God! The nation will call us blessed, and heaven will open and war on our behalf! We make a declaration that good health, wealth, and wisdom is our portion. We bind the hands of the enemy and shut his mouth and loose the blood of Jesus and the blessing that makes rich and adds no sorrow!

Now, God, we ask that you break us out. We seal this prayer with the blood of Jesus. Again, we bind the enemy's hands and shut his mouth. Satan, we rebuke you, the blood of Jesus is against you and no weapon formed against us shall prosper in the name of Jesus. We bind backlash, retaliation, and destruction. We loose the blood of Jesus and the blessings that makes rich and adds no sorrow with it (Proverbs 10:22).

We thank You in advance for what is already done. We thank you that soul ties are broken and breakthrough has occurred. We bless you for delivering our bodies, minds, and soul. We thank You for freedom and a long, healthy, and prosperous life, in Jesus name we pray, Amen.

Thank you for purchasing this book! I pray this book blesses you abundantly.

In "Break Through, Sis," Dr. Karen Ratliff offers insight on how to receive the promises of God. She provides practical words of wisdom, tips, tools, and resources to intentionally assist with the pursuit of freedom by breaking through trials, tribulations, and troubles. "Break Through, Sis," will ignite a desire to become free of what is holding you back and to run towards what God has in store for you.

www.ingramcontent.com/pod-product-compliance
Lightning Source LLC
LaVergne TN
LVHW051508080426
835509LV00017B/1979